THE INDIE AUTHOR MINDSET

HOW CHANGING YOUR WAY OF THINKING CAN TRANSFORM YOUR WRITING CAREER

ADAM CROFT

I've had a lot of interesting conversations over the course of the last few years since I started to really concentrate on my self publishing career. I'm fortunate enough to be asked to speak at conferences around the world, and one of those opportunities comes to mind more easily than some of the others. It was the London Book Fair and I had just finished a Q&A session for Amazon. I was approached by a new writer who asked me how much of my day was spent writing. I told her that I tended to split my day into two parts: I wrote in the morning and took care of business in the afternoon. She nodded her head, as if I had just confirmed her worst suspicions, and then told me that I wasn't really a full-time writer.

True story.

I don't know the name of that writer, but I would

lay long odds that she never had the success that she thought she was due. It is almost always the case these days that the successful independent authors are those who are prepared to combine their creativity with a willingness to roll up their sleeves and get stuck into the marketing, advertising and audience building that is necessary to move things to the next level.

We have to treat our writing as a business. That means that we need to be prepared to invest in ourselves, our books and the support network that will enable us to reach out around the world to find new readers and convert them into lifetime fans. Adam understands this. He was one of the first authors to enrol in my Ads for Authors course and has since become one of our biggest success stories. He has demonstrated that apart from writing page turning books that his readers enjoy, he's also prepared to treat his calling as a business and act accordingly.

This book sets out how authors should think smart about their indie careers. If writers go into this brave new world of publishing with the right frame of mind and the right foundations for their businesses, more often than not the rest will fall into place.

There's never been a better time to be a writer, with the caveat that you need to be prepared to learn from the people who have gone before you. This is a great chance to do that. Good luck and happy reading.

Mark Dawson
  Salisbury, July 2018

With more than a million books sold to date, Adam Croft is one of the most successful independently published authors in the world, and one of the biggest selling authors of the past few years.

Following his 2015 worldwide bestseller *Her Last Tomorrow*, his psychological thrillers were bought by Thomas & Mercer, an imprint of Amazon Publishing. Prior to the Amazon deal, *Her Last Tomorrow* sold more than 150,000 copies across all platforms and became one of the bestselling books of the year, reaching the top 10 in the overall Amazon Kindle chart and peaking at number 12 in the combined paperback fiction and non-fiction chart.

His Knight & Culverhouse crime thriller series has sold more than 250,000 copies worldwide, with his Kempston Hardwick mystery books being adapted as audio plays starring some of the biggest names in British TV.

In 2016, the *Knight & Culverhouse Box Set* reached storewide number 1 in Canada, knocking J.K. Rowling's *Harry Potter and the Cursed Child* off the top spot only weeks after *Her Last Tomorrow* was also number

1 in Canada. The new edition of *Her Last Tomorrow* also reached storewide number 1 in Australia over Christmas 2016.

During the summer of 2016, two of Adam's books hit the USA Today bestseller list only weeks apart, making them two of the most-purchased books in the United States over the summer.

In February 2017, *Only The Truth* became a worldwide bestseller, reaching storewide number 1 at both Amazon US and Amazon UK, making it the bestselling book in the world at that moment in time. The same day, Amazon's overall Author Rankings placed Adam as the most widely read author in the world, with J.K. Rowling in second place.

Adam has been featured on BBC television, BBC Radio 4, BBC Radio 5 Live, the BBC World Service, The Guardian, The Huffington Post, The Bookseller and a number of other news and media outlets.

In March 2018, Adam was conferred as an Honorary Doctor of Arts, the highest academic qualification in the UK, by the University of Bedfordshire in recognition of his achievements.

Adam presents the regular crime fiction podcast *Partners in Crime* with fellow bestselling author Robert Daws.

facebook.com/adamcroftbooks

twitter.com/adamcroft

I got it wrong for years.

When I first started writing and publishing almost a decade ago, there wasn't the wealth of information available that there is now.

Today's experts and visionaries had, for the most part, not even started on their own journeys into independent publishing.

The Kindle had only just become available in the UK and the industry was still extremely young and far from finding its feet.

Now that I've been able to enjoy extraordinary success, I feel it's only right to help those who are at the start of their own publishing journey.

I often lurk about in indie author Facebook groups and regularly invite authors to contact me if they have any questions or need any advice or help. Giving back is something that means a lot to me.

But, more often than not, the problems that other authors encounter are the same. The more I think about it, the more I realise that the vast majority of authors' issues and stumbling blocks are due to an incorrect way of thinking.

Being an indie author is hard. You have to be both creative and business-minded. It requires a totally different way of thinking to the conventional, and you will often need to apply a seemingly illogical or frightening thought process in order to succeed.

But, if you can nail the indie author mindset, succeed you will.

It'll still be difficult. It'll still take time. But you *will* get there.

Mindset might seem like a vague term, or the sort of thing a self-help guru might bang on about. But it's much more than that.

This book aims to put you in the right frame of mind to succeed in your indie author career. It'll teach you fundamental principles on which you can base all of your decisions as you move forward. Mindset will be the foundation for your future success.

This isn't a book about marketing. It isn't a book about advertising. But it is a guide to perhaps the most important but often-overlooked aspect of your career as an author, and one which will shape everything you do from here on in.

In this book, I'll show you the three primary

mindsets you need to adopt, along with practical tips and real-life examples from my own career.

The book will build on itself as you work your way through. Established authors will see the early chapters as fairly basic, and new writers might begin to get overwhelmed towards the end. That's absolutely fine. I've tried to pitch this book in such a way that everyone will get something out of it.

If at any time you feel the book is going over stuff you already know or — conversely — is a little daunting, please hang in there.

You'll come away from reading this book feeling energised, reinvigorated and — I hope — inspired.

We're going to have a lot of fun. But first we need to do some groundwork.

WHAT IS SELF-PUBLISHING?

WHAT SELF-PUBLISHING
IS NOT

This might seem like a rather odd way to start a chapter on what self-publishing is, but it's a lot easier to dispel the myths first, believe me.

There's a reason this chapter is right at the start of the book, and that's because I want to make sure as many new writers as possible see it. It's incredibly important to me.

I spend large parts of my life trying to convince people that their understanding of self-publishing is false.

If a company or individual charges you to publish your book, it is NOT self-publishing.

Nor is the company a traditional publisher. These outfits should be avoided at all costs. I really can't say that strongly enough. My word processor doesn't have a quadruple-bold function, but if it did I'd use it.

There are only two forms of legitimate publishing, and the above model is not one of them.

In **self-publishing**, you are both the author <u>and</u> the publishing company. The only costs you need to incur are your own time. Having said that, I strongly recommend hiring a cover designer and editor — more on that later.

In short, though, if someone offers you a 'self-publishing service' or charges you money to publish your book, run as fast as you can. Don't touch those guys with a bargepole. They charge extortionate amounts of money for something which is not only easy to do, but is completely free.

I've lost count of the number of times writers have contacted me to tell me about the problems they've had with self-publishing companies. One author paid over £20,000 to a company to publish his book and was surprised that they did no promotional work for him and he sold almost no copies. I wasn't surprised. That company had no incentive to do a thing for him in terms of promotion. Why would they? They had his twenty grand and had moved on to the next sucker. A publisher will have a vested interest in the success of your books.

That's because in the other half of the industry,

traditional publishing, the publisher pays you. They will (in most cases) offer you a cash advance and pay a royalty on sales thereafter. The advance is the publisher putting their money where their mouth is. It is their incentive to ensure your books are marketed and sell well. Without that success, they won't recoup their advance. If the book doesn't sell, you keep the money they've paid you. They need your book to sell.

There is one small caveat I must add. Some very good and reputable publishers, such as Bookouture and Bloodhound (amongst others) don't offer advances to authors. However, the key is that they don't charge them a penny either. The onus is still on them to make your books a success because they plough thousands of pounds into cover designers and editors, as well as marketing budgets.

And that's the key: a publisher will invest **their** money and **their** time — not yours.

It must be said, of course, that even authors published by traditional publishers will *still* have to do a large part of the marketing themselves. This is expected of all authors nowadays, so even the traditional route won't absolve you of your marketing duties.

Please, **please**, PLEASE avoid any company that charges for 'self publishing' or any publisher who wants you to stump up even a penny of your money to get your book published.

There are 'new model' companies who will work with you to get your book published and share in the profits with you, and some of them are even run by friends of mine.

These 'new model' companies aren't dishonest — I just honestly believe that with some time and applied knowledge, any author can do the things they do and enjoy a greater share of their own income off the back of it.

However, if you're dead set on guaranteed publication and don't want to learn how to build a successful indie career on your own, then: a) this book probably isn't for you, and b) you can find a list of authentic, bona-fide companies vetted by the Alliance of Independent Authors at https://croft.link/ALLiVettedServices

If you're in any doubt whatsoever about whether the publisher or company you're involved with is legitimate, please email me at mindset@adamcroft.net. All emails will go straight to me and I'll let you know if you're on the right path. What's more, I won't charge you a penny.

WHAT SELF-PUBLISHING IS

Just to confuse matters further, I'm going to make a small confession that could throw everything into disarray.

I don't like calling it 'self-publishing', although I will, for various reasons (not least a bit of variety) refer to it as both self-publishing and indie publishing throughout this book.

The reality is that there's no 'self' about it. Independent publishing (which is what I call it, and is the term I encourage others to use) involves more people than just yourself. Remember what I said in the previous chapter about you being the author *and* the publishing company? Not many publishing companies consist of just one person.

Now, I'm not suggesting you hire a tower block and fifty interns — far from it — but you are going to have to rely on other people if your independent publishing journey is going to be a success. For instance, my books would not be possible without my cover designer and three editors at the very least. And that's without counting all the others who are invaluable to me: friends who count as sounding boards, people who run book promotion websites, contacts at vendors, festival organisers and just about everyone else I come into contact with through my work.

Please don't be put off by that, though. Bear in mind that I'm over eight years into my career and sell huge numbers of books. If you're just starting out, all you need is a cover designer and an editor.

'But I can do that myself!' I hear you say. Sure you can. I'm not bad at cooking, but I don't take my friends out to a swanky restaurant and quickly pop into the kitchen to rustle them up an omelette. There are guys there who make far better food than I do, and my friends expect far more when they walk into that restaurant than a plate of sloppy eggs I threw together inside three minutes.

From the very start of my career, my mantra has always been that my books should be absolutely indistinguishable from traditionally published books.

Readers, generally, don't care who publishes a book. They do care, however, that it has a great cover and is free from spelling and grammatical errors.

But please, **please** don't attempt to design your own covers or do your own editing.

Do you know what my last two jobs were before I became a full-time author? I was a designer and an editor. And even *I* wouldn't dream of designing my own covers or editing my own books. And there are two very good reasons for that:

1. Book cover design is VERY different from any other design

It doesn't matter how good you are with Photoshop or Canva. If you are not an experienced (and I mean 5 years+ full-time) book cover designer, please don't try to design your own covers. They'll stand out a mile, and not in a good way. If you want readers to take you seriously, you need to take yourself seriously.

2. You cannot edit your own books

I'm afraid this is just pure scientific fact. When you look at a sentence or a word, you *know* what that word or sentence is meant to say and your brain presents it to you in that way. Only an editor with fresh eyes on the text will be able to spot those errors. Besides which, editors have a huge number of benefits on top of that which will be invaluable to your books.

The message is simple: readers won't take your books seriously if you don't present them seriously. If you want people to part with their hard-earned money and buy your book, you need to show that you've made the same commitment. You owe it to your readers and yourself to give them the best possible product.

But what if you haven't got any money?

I had less than no money when I started writing. In no other industry would you set up a business and expect to invest absolutely no money. How many shoe shops do you think you could open with no money? Not many landlords would let you use their shopfront without paying rent. And not many people would go into your shop if you decided to paint your own sign on the front with a pack of crayons you found down the back of your sofa.

Distinguishing between expenditure and investment is a facet of the business mindset that we'll come to later in this book, but for now don't worry yourself about it too much. There are far more fun things to talk about first...

SUMMARY POINTS

- **Understand the limitations of your abilities and be honest about what these are.**

- Hire professionals to carry out the jobs you can't do. Your books will thank you for it.
- Understand that you're a business owner and some form of investment is essential.

MANAGING YOUR
EXPECTATIONS

THIS IS GOING TO BE HARD

I get a lot of emails from a lot of authors who've read stories of my success and want to emulate it. That's always great to hear and I always do my best to help nudge them a little closer to that point, but it's important that all authors — at whatever stage of their careers — are able to manage their expectations.

The sad truth is that the average traditionally published author earns less than £11,000 ($15,700) per year. That's less than the National Minimum Wage here in the UK (about £14,000 [$20,000] a year or £1,166 [$1,665] a month at the time of writing).

Bear in mind that those authors are the ones with a traditional, bona fide contract from a reputable publisher, who've each been the lucky one picked out of a pool of tens of thousands of submissions and reached the 'holy grail' of the writing world.

Of course, it's now generally accepted that a traditional contract isn't the holy grail at all, but that there are other, much more lucrative and successful routes to take.

It is entirely possible for you to be an author and to earn a lot of money — but only if you have the right mindset and put in the necessary amount of work. No, not everyone can be in the 1%, but the only reason it is 1% is because that's how many people have adapted their mindset and decided to change and grow as an author. You, too, could do that. Independent publishing is a super-viable business model, but you need to approach it with the right mindset.

I'm quite open about the financial freedom my success has brought me. I earn six figures a year from my writing and my wife has been able to leave her job and now works full-time doing the back-office stuff for my books. But I'm well aware that I'm in the top 1% and that the vast majority of authors won't earn anywhere near what I do. Having said that, some good friends of mine make six figures a month, so even I'm not at the top of the scale.

Self-publishing probably won't make you rich. Then again, all I ever wanted to do was earn just about enough to be able to do it full-time. The rest has been sheer good fortune, but I'm not complaining. It was hard work. It'll be hard work for you, too. At times it'll drain your soul. But it's still, hands down, the best thing I ever did in my career.

It's going to be a long road. You're going to have to change the way you've thought about things for years. You're going to have to make major adjustments to fundamental beliefs you may have held your entire life. But if you want to become a full-time independent author, earning decent money doing the thing you love, having complete control over everything you do — it'll be worth every drop of blood, sweat and tears.

You'll have to spend time doing some incredibly boring and soul-destroying things like bookkeeping, logging data and organising marketing campaigns. There'll be days when you log into your sales dashboard and see that you sold no books yesterday. There'll be times when you want to chuck it all in and forget everything. Trust me. I've been there. Many times.

But I can promise you this: you will have a lot of fun.

"Fear is good. Like self-doubt, fear is an indicator. Fear tells us what we have to do ... So if you're paralyzed with fear, it's a good sign. It shows you what you have to do."

STEVEN PRESSFIELD, THE WAR OF ART.

SUMMARY POINTS

- **Buckle up. It's damn hard, but it's super possible. Let's enjoy the ride.**

PART ONE

THE PROFESSIONAL MINDSET

PROFESSIONALISM

WHAT IS PROFESSIONALISM?

People often ask me how long I've been a writer.

It might sound like a simple question, but there are a number of ways I could answer it.

I've been writing ever since I was a child. I've always enjoyed writing stories. I remember being sent out of class when I was about six years old, and subsequently writing a story about pirates for my younger brother. If I remember correctly, it was his birthday that day.

I recall writing the first episode of a new TV soap opera I'd dreamt up. I was probably about eleven or so, and typed the whole thing up on an old Smith Corona typewriter my mother let me use.

But was I a writer? Who knows?

I've been earning money from my writing for over a decade. For the first few years, it was nowhere near a full-time wage, though. At which point did I become a writer?

People often refer to the point where I turned 'professional' as perhaps the definitive moment that I became a writer. But that begs another question…

What is *professional*?

Even the Oxford English Dictionary doesn't help. It defines *professional* as:

> A person engaged in a specified activity, especially a sport, as a **main paid occupation** rather than as a pastime,

which rather indicates that I only became a professional writer once *Her Last Tomorrow* took off. However, the very next line in the OED offers an alternative definition:

> A person competent or skilled in a particular activity.

Was I competent before *Her Last Tomorrow* was released? I certainly hope so. What about when I wrote that imaginary soap opera episode? Was I skilled? What about the pirate story when I was six?

The lines, as you can see, are rather blurred to say the least.

And that's because professionalism is about more than just money and skill.

It's about mindset.

THE PROFESSIONAL MINDSET

In *The War of Art*, Steven Pressfield defines this perfectly:

> The word amateur comes from the Latin root meaning "to love." The conventional interpretation is that the amateur pursues his calling out of love, while the pro does it for money. Not the way I see it. In my view, the amateur does not love the game enough. If he did, he would not pursue it as a sideline, distinct from his "real" vocation.

Professionalism is about dedication. It's about turning up, putting in the hours and getting the work done.

It's about attitude. It's about approaching your writing career in a professional manner and not treating it as a hobby and pastime.

It's about respect. If you don't show your writing career the same respect as you'd show any other job or career, you're missing the point entirely.

Without the professional mindset, you're doomed to failure.

SUMMARY POINTS

- **Professionalism is about mindset, dedication, attitude and respect.**

You don't need me to teach you how to be a professional. You are one.

I'm going to presume that you either currently have, or have at some point had, a paying job. If that's the case, you're a professional.

You know what it is to get up in the morning for a vocation. You know all about having to do something in order to earn money and live. You know about responsibility and professional respect.

But you've likely not considered transferring those skills and experiences over into your writing life.

WHAT MAKES YOU A PROFESSIONAL?

As you'll know from your own experience of work, the factors which defined it as a job were:

- Commitment of effort
- Commitment of time
- Commitment to prioritise
- High stakes and dependence
- Separation of identity
- Long-term mastering of a craft
- The expectation of financial reward

Let's break those down one by one.

COMMITMENT OF EFFORT

By turning up for work each day, you agree to give your job your full commitment. You put your best effort in, knowing it'll be rewarded in the long run.

COMMITMENT OF TIME

You arrive on time and you do the hours you're contracted to do.

COMMITMENT TO PRIORITISE

While you're at work, it is your primary focus. A professional wouldn't spend the day browsing Facebook in their office.

HIGH STAKES AND DEPENDENCE

We all depend on our jobs to provide income for us and our families, and most people have a deep fear of losing their job.

SEPARATION OF IDENTITY

When you're at work, you're a different person. You have a work identity which is separate from your home or social identity.

LONG-TERM MASTERING OF A CRAFT

Whatever your job, you're likely to get better at it the longer you do it. A carpenter will get more skilled and precise as the years go by. A customer services assistant will improve their patience and customer-facing skills with every year.

THE EXPECTATION OF FINANCIAL REWARD

This goes without saying. One of the fundamental aspects of your job is that you get paid for it.

Are you starting to understand what I'm getting at here?

This is the way in which you should approach your writing career.

Being a professional writer is not something that happens to you. It is something you make happen.

It is an active choice to give your career the dedication and commitment it requires. And you already know exactly how to do that.

SUMMARY POINTS

- **You already know how to approach things with professionalism.**
- **Professionalism requires commitment of effort, time and priority, as well as being able to separate yourself from your work and dedicate yourself to mastering your craft.**

People often ask me what advice I'd give to writers. My answer is always the same six words: **Ass on chair, fingers on keyboard.**

There's no escaping the facts. In today's market-place, you need to be a productive writer to be a successful writer.

Of course, there are anomalies. But if you want to maximise your chances of success, you need to get productive. Easier said than done, right?

In the early stages of putting this book together, one of my beta readers commented that it takes them a year to write a book. My heart sank a little.

'Slow' writers aren't necessarily going to be unsuccessful. Harper Lee's currently knocking out a book every fifty-five years (except she's not any more because she's dead). It didn't do her any harm. Apart from the dying bit, I mean.

But we can't all have a Pulitzer Prize winner and one of the greatest novels of all time with our first book. For us mere mortals, we need to be productive.

There's a reason why the most successful indie authors pump out books at a rate of knots. It's because it works.

Put it this way: a voracious reader will easily demolish your book in a day. There's no way even the most productive author could write a book that fast, so the painful truth is **you'll never write quickly enough**.

That's not meant to dishearten you. My point is that you can always write faster. The more books you have out, the more money you'll make and the easier your job will get.

GET IN THE HABIT

Writing is a muscle that needs to be exercised.

If you hadn't done any physical exercise in years and I asked you to give me a hundred sit-ups and go on a five-mile run, would you be able to do it? Probably not. But if you regularly kept fit you'd work your way up to that and probably go far beyond.

Writing is the same.

Writing every day is absolutely crucial. That muscle needs to be worked regularly in order for it to get easier. Just writing in your spare time isn't enough — you need to dedicate time every day to your pursuit.

WRITE NOW, EDIT LATER

Many 'slow' writers have a tendency to edit as they go along. This will **always** slow the process down an awful lot and is never a good idea.

You should always get the first draft down as quickly as possible. This has a number of advantages.

Firstly, you now have a book. Sure, it needs editing, but it's a book. It's done. The hardest part is finished.

Editing as you go along will slow you down. Editing after you've got a finished draft will be a whole lot quicker.

DON'T AIM FOR PERFECTION

Forget about making everything perfect. It won't happen. Perfection doesn't exist in this game.

Books are subjective. One person will love your book and the next person will hate it. There's literally no point in trying to achieve your own personal ideal of perfection, as it might be the complete opposite of what your reader wants. Get that first draft written, then edit it to make it into a good book, then release it.

Anything else will slow down the process, lengthen the time it takes you to get your book to market and will, ultimately, cost you money.

IF THERE'S A WILL, THERE'S A WAY

'That's all well and good,' I hear you say, *'but I work full-time and have children!'*

Don't worry. I get it. I really do. And that's why productivity hacks and 'getting things done' are things I'm passionate about.

I know many authors who've been fortunate enough to throw in the towel and go all-in with their writing. It's enabled them to suddenly 'switch on' and give everything, which can have superb results.

Imagine being able to suddenly write a book every month or two, or to have hours a day to dedicate to marketing and advertising.

Most people, of course, won't have that luxury. We all have commitments in our life which will get in the way of our writing. That's perfectly natural, right?

If you read the previous two chapters on professionalism, you might be starting to see where I'm going with this.

By being a professional at whatever you currently do, be it a secretary, doctor or home keeper, you prioritise it and you find the time. Your writing should be no different.

If you really want to earn a full-time living from your writing and for it to provide a secure future for you and your family, you need to make sacrifices now and find the time that your writing career needs.

I know this will probably not be the answer you want, but there's absolutely no way around it. If you could just write a book in your own time, put it out, do very little and sell millions of copies everyone would be doing it. And believe me, lots of people are giving it a good old go with that approach. Oddly enough, it tends not to work.

There are things you can do, though, to find the time and to make that time more productive for you.

GET UP EARLIER

I know this is easier said than done. At the time of writing I have a young son who likes to wake me up at five o'clock in the morning by jumping on my face, and that's more than early enough for me.

But it's amazing what you can get done in an extra hour or half an hour before everyone else is awake. Many people are at their most creative in the morning, so take advantage of that. A few hundred words extra each day can make a huge difference.

For example, if I've planned what I'm going to write properly I can easily put out 1,000 words in half an hour. If we want to be a little less ambitious, let's say 500.

Getting up half an hour earlier in the mornings is something anyone can do. If you get up half an hour earlier every morning, those 500 words a day equate to 3,500 a week, or 15,000 words a month that you wouldn't have had otherwise.

If you get up an hour earlier and manage 1,000 extra words a day, you'll have 30,000 words in a month. That's an entire novel in just three months, without having to cut down on any other commitments (except that bit of sleep).

CUT THE CRAP

We all waste time. Even I do. People often ask me how I get so much done, and I always feel an awkward inward curl as I think about how much time I spend playing Candy Crush or watching car crash videos on YouTube.

No-one's denying you a bit of downtime, but there's always plenty we can cut back on. Think about how much TV you watch. Could you knock half an hour off that each night? What about time spent on social media?

Pro tip: I highly recommend the smartphone app *Moment*. It tracks how much screen time your smartphone sees each day and whether it was more or less than the day before. The results can be absolutely frightening. For instance, I had a *very* busy day yesterday and don't recall having spent any time playing on my phone, but Moment tells me I spent 5 hours and 32 minutes on my iPhone, an increase of 2 hours and 18 minutes from the day before. That's a HUGE amount of time that could be spent writing.

THE POMODORO TECHNIQUE

The Pomodoro Technique is a productivity system designed by Francesco Crillo in the late 1980s and, for reasons I'm still unable to fathom, is named after the Italian word for *tomato*.

The theory is that you concentrate on doing one task (in this case, writing) for 25 minutes, followed by a short break of a few minutes. After four sessions, you can treat yourself to a longer break of fifteen to twenty minutes.

GTD (GETTING THINGS DONE)

This is a concept developed by David Allen (no, not the Irish comedian) which says that you should start and finish all your smallest tasks straight away, then break up the big tasks into smaller ones, which you should then start on. The idea is that your big tasks then seem less daunting.

TIMEBOXING

This is similar to The Pomodoro Technique, but is a version that I've tweaked to suit my own work patterns. Essentially, I write for twenty minutes (or half an hour), then have twenty minutes or half an hour to do something fun, before repeating the cycle again.

This might sound counterintuitive — after all, aren't I then only getting four hours work done in an eight hour day?

Yes, but that's often more than I'd get done anyway. If I forced myself to sit down and work for eight hours solid, I'd get distracted by social media, making tea and just about anything else to avoid work, and might end up doing an hour or two at most.

Either way, it's crucial that you find something that works for you. We can't stretch the days out to be thirty hours long, but we can easily stretch a whole lot more into twenty-four hours than we might think possible.

SUMMARY POINTS

- Professionals find the time and prioritise what needs to be done to achieve their goals.
- Getting up half an hour earlier can yield huge productivity results.
- Be honest with yourself about the time you waste. Can you cut back on TV? Social media? Candy Crush?
- Try the Pomodoro Technique — write for 25 minutes, then rest for five.
- Get Things Done by breaking big tasks into their smaller components.
- Try timeboxing. Find a length of time that works for you.

ENCOUNTERING DOUBT

BELIEVING IN YOURSELF

Self-doubt can be an ally. This is because it serves as an indicator of aspiration. It reflects love, love of something we dream of doing, and desire, desire to do it. If you find yourself asking yourself (and your friends), "Am I really a writer? Am I really an artist?" chances are you are.

STEVEN PRESSFIELD, THE WAR OF ART.

One of the biggest problems to plague writers is self-doubt. And all writers get it to some degree.

Self-doubt, put simply, is a lack of confidence in your own abilities. It isn't necessarily linked to self-esteem, either, as many people seem to think. People with plenty of self-esteem can easily be plagued with self-doubt.

I think I have more self-doubt now than I did

when I started writing a decade ago. That's probably due to the fact that I now have increased pressures because of the success I've enjoyed, but every time I write a book I do so completely convinced that this book is the one that'll get me 'found out'.

It's classic imposter syndrome, a term coined in 1978 by two clinical psychologists, Pauline R. Clance and Suzanne A. Imes. It's a recognised psychological disorder which affects both men and women in equal proportions, with sufferers remaining convinced their achievements were entirely down to luck or timing and that they've deceived others into thinking they're more talented than they really are.

> A successful person is one who can lay a firm foundation with the bricks that others throw at him or her.
> David Brinkley

Karyl McBride Ph.D., writing in Psychology Today in 2011, split self-doubt into two parts: the inability to give oneself credit, and feeling like an imposter.

INABILITY TO GIVE ONESELF CREDIT

This might sound pretty self-explanatory, but actually goes a lot deeper than you might expect. In the article, McBride states, 'If raised by a narcissistic parent, an adult child will invariably be fearful that they will grow up to be narcissistic themselves. This makes it difficult to give self credit for fear of being arrogant or behaving like a narcissist'.

Woah, easy there. No-one's suggesting you were raised by narcissistic parents, but I think her point still stands. Many of us struggle to give ourselves credit for fear of seeming arrogant, without casting aspersions towards our parents. In Britain, we're especially afflicted with this as it's historically been seen as culturally unacceptable to brag. Fortunately for us, it's also a cultural obligation to say 'Nuts to that' at least twice a day.

McBride goes on to say, 'This means that if you have accomplishments and have worked hard in life, it is real and you can give yourself credit for this. You don't need to brag, but you can give yourself that credit where credit is due.'

So, there you go. A proper doctor said it. Believe it now?

IMPOSTER SYNDROME

In the same article, McBride describes imposter syndrome as 'the inability to accept and claim accomplishments no matter what level of success, even with hard-won achievements because there is an irrational fear that you don't deserve the success or maybe you are just a fraud'.

I've interviewed dozens of famous authors for the *Partners in Crime* podcast which I co-present, and they all, without doubt, express some form of imposter syndrome. It seems to be 'the creative disease' which spurs us all on and compels us to create something bigger and better next time.

There are some common signs of imposter syndrome which I'm sure most (if not all) writers will recognise:

- Fear of failure
- Perfectionism
- Not believing praise
- An unhealthy focus on criticism
- Attributing all successes externally

Let's look at those one at a time.

FEAR OF FAILURE

> Defeat is not the worst of failures. Not to have tried is the true failure.
>
> GEORGE EDWARD WOODBERRY

We all fear failure. It's not an irrational fear, either. After all, who actually *wants* to fail? But what if I told you there was no such thing as failure?

Think about this for a moment. When you do something, it can either be a success or a failure, right? Wrong. That would be a very negative way of thinking about anything other than outright success. It's all about expectations and measuring success. The only way you can fail is to quit.

So what if, rather than failures, there are only successes and learning experiences? I've had *many* 'failures'. Far more than I've had successes. But you only need a few successes, and every experience that wasn't a success has taught me something. Every time something doesn't work, I sit back (after a long time of shouting, screaming and sulking) and analyse what went wrong. What could I do better next time? Was it something I did or did external circumstances conspire against me?

Fear of failure should not stop you doing something you want to do. One of my maxims in life is that I'd far rather regret doing something than regret not doing it. When I'm on my deathbed, I don't want to have a single 'what if' going through my mind. I'd much rather think about things that didn't quite work out rather than wonder what might have happened.

PERFECTIONISM

I'm not the first person to have said this — no

writer ever feels that the execution of a book lives up to the idea for that book. The execution always falls short.

STEPHEN KING

To some degree, all creatives are perfectionists. But any artist knows the next brush stroke — just to add a bit more blue — could ruin the whole portrait. At some point, it has to be left alone and called 'finished'.

No book ever feels finished. No piece of creative work does. But **you** have to call time on it and move on. Get that first draft written. **Don't** edit a word until the whole book is completed in first draft form. Then do your self-edit and hand it on to a professional editor. Let them do what they're good at. No-one ever writes a book and thinks 'Yeah that book's perfect'.

NOT BELIEVING PRAISE

Build your self-esteem by recalling all the ways you have succeeded, and your brain will be filled with images of you making your achievements happen again and again. Give yourself permission to toot your own horn, and don't wait for anyone to praise you.

JACK CANFIELD

For a long time, every time anyone said anything nice about me I'd tell them they were wrong. I'd make some self-disparaging remark about how it was all down to luck, or that they must be mistaken. I soon realised that not only was this rude, it was also incredibly unhelpful.

Learning to accept praise is all about growing as a person. Accept that people like you and your work and give yourself the credit you're due.

AN UNHEALTHY FOCUS ON CRITICISM

People react to criticism in different ways, and my way is definitely to come out fighting.

DAVID BECKHAM

We've all done it. A friend makes a perfectly inno-cent remark — perhaps in jest — and we stew on it for weeks and months. We overanalyse what they say, what they do and generally beat ourselves up about something completely innocent.

You're better than that.

If you've already published a book I would wager that you check your reviews fairly often. I did so for years. I'd look at the latest reviews on my books on Amazon and analyse everything that was said. To this day, I don't remember any of the positive ones but I can remember every word of the negative reviews.

That's ridiculous. I've got thousands of reviews and maybe a couple of dozen are negative. The vast, vast majority are overwhelmingly positive and readers seem to love my books. But despite the clear evidence to the contrary, my brain still wants to focus on the negativity.

This is remarkably common, but there's a fix for it.

Two or three years ago, I stopped reading reviews. And I mean completely stopped. I'll occasionally have a glance at the overall star rating on Amazon, which sits at the top of the page next to the book's title. But I **never** scroll down and read what reviewers have said. Why? **Because it helps no-one**.

If a book has an average of 2 or 3 stars out of five (which has never happened yet) I'll know I've done something wrong and should scroll down to see if there's any constructive criticism in the Amazon reviews (Pro tip: There almost invariably won't be). Otherwise, I just take the overall score as a measure of how much readers liked my book on average — which is exactly what it's designed for.

An early reader of this book commented that this is fine for me to say after selling over a million books, but that new writers will not seriously consider this advice.

I'd go so far as to say that new writers should seriously consider this advice **even more** than established writers. With over a million books sold, I have enough 'other' validation to not take a lone negative review too seriously. New writers don't have that luxury, and are even more susceptible to being swayed by a negative review.

But what if someone writes something false or inaccurate or gives away spoilers?! I hear you say. And I'm afraid that's completely irrelevant. We're dealing with Amazon here, and Amazon won't remove reviews when authors ask them to. In the past I've taken this up with the people who run KDP, as well as publishing directors at Amazon and they just don't remove reviews unless their automated algorithms deem them to be falsified. (And anyone who follows the industry closely knows that this algorithm is about as sophisticated and accurate as dropping a jelly bean out of a helicopter and seeing which author's bowl it lands in.)

Trust me on this. I've had people leaving reviews on the wrong book and Amazon still won't remove them. I've had people reviewing goddamn kettles and toasters and leaving the reviews on my books accidentally, and Amazon still won't remove them. I've had people giving away the killer in the massive bold header of their review and — yes, you guessed it — Amazon still won't remove them.

Don't sweat the small stuff. Ignore reviews, have a look at where your time is best spent and get on with writing more great books.

Don't get caught in a downward spiral of negativity. You won't convince or win over a reader who doesn't like your work, but the more time you spend trying to do so, the less time you're spending on the people who do like your work and want to buy more of it.

BUT IF YOU DO...

I'm a realist. I know a large proportion of you will ignore this advice and read your reviews. I did the same — for many years.

When you come across a negative review you'll likely feel disheartened. We already know that. But there are things you can do to make yourself feel better.

READ OTHER PEOPLE'S BAD REVIEWS

There's nothing that soothes the soul quite like a bit of schadenfreude. Go and take a look at the 1-star reviews on some of your favourite books, or on some of the greatest books of all time.

Charles Dickens's *Great Expectations* was reviewed

by Alan Jones on Amazon in an epic consisting of just one word: 'Boring'. P Yates on Amazon describes Harper Lee's classic *To Kill A Mockingbird* as 'really tedious'. *Don Quixote*, by Miguel de Cervantes, is often cited as the greatest book of all time. Not according to Chedley on Amazon, though, whose review calls it 'Utter rubbish, As a classic I thought I would like this but it was just too silly and very boring. Was glad when I finished it. Kept reading so at least I could say that I gave it a chance. Waste of my time.'

My point is this: Books are subjective. Not everyone is going to like *any* book.

READ THE GOOD REVIEWS

Go on. All of them. Keep reading until you believe them. And take a look at that overall score: you'll probably find there are far more good reviews than there are bad ones, in which case you can feel vindicated that your writing **is** good and people **do** like it.

I've released over twenty books, have two *USA Today* bestsellers under my belt, as well as having achieved several storewide number-one bestsellers. I've sold more than 1.5 million books, have been translated into multiple languages, had TV and film companies begging at my doorstep and have been awarded the highest academic achievement in Britain — an honorary Doctorate of Arts — in recognition of my services to literature. And I *still* feel like a fraud.

I feel like it's all been down to luck and good timing. Even writing the paragraph above was painful for me as it felt like I was bragging or being deceitful. As I typed the last part I was thinking 'An *honorary* Doctorate of Arts! You didn't even *earn* it!'. I'm still convinced all the times I've hit the number one spot they must have been quiet weeks with even worse books than mine being released.

My point is this: the self-doubt will never go away, whether it's the classic form of self-doubt or imposter syndrome. You simply have to learn to deal with it, overcome it and get on with things despite it being there in the background. Like any bully, if you ignore it it'll eventually pipe down and disappear.

There are, however, things you can do to help improve self-doubt and imposter syndrome:

WRITE A SUCCESS DIARY

Wait. Come back. Please. This isn't as daft as it sounds.

On days when I feel like I'm a nobody, I sit down and I think back ten years, or even five. Where did I want to be five or ten years later? I wanted to be earning full-time money from writing, living in a nice house, driving a nice car and to have a solid foundation on which to build the rest of my career. Without exception, I've achieved all that. So why do I still feel like I've achieved nothing?

What I'm lacking is perspective. I'm judging myself by *today*'s standards, rather than those goals I set myself years ago. Only by recognising that I've achieved my goals, and then setting new ones, can I feel as though I'm getting somewhere.

It's fine to want more. In fact, it's healthy from a career point of view. But you also need to be able to look back and see where you *were* in order to appreciate where you *are*.

Once a year, write down your goals for the future. Jot down where you want to be this time next year, as well as in five or ten years' time. You might just be surprised at how far you've come.

KEEP A SUCCESS SCRAPBOOK

This can be physical or digital, but make sure you log your successes and achievements. Print out all those lovely emails you get from readers. Take screenshots of your number 1 rankings. If you win a competition or get an award, pop it in the scrapbook. Whatever makes you feel good about your writing needs logging.

When you're feeling self-doubt creep in again

(and it will) open the scrapbook and motivate your-self to pick your feet up and get going again.

SUMMARY POINTS

- Understand that self-doubt and imposter syndrome are natural and very common.
- Understand that even the most successful authors are plagued by self-doubt.
- Realise that self-doubt can drive you forward rather than hold you backwards.
- Don't edit as you go — perfectionism is unattainable, and that's fine.
- Accept praise and use it to build your self-confidence.
- Ignore criticism and bad reviews. There'll often not be much you can take from it.
- Write a success diary to track your achievements and put them in perspective.
- Keep a success scrapbook to motivate yourself when self-doubt strikes.
- Judge yourself by looking at your historic goals, not by today's standards.

THE POWER OF OTHERS

WHEN TO LISTEN AND
WHEN NOT TO LISTEN

A couple of years ago I got an email from an author who wanted my help. He couldn't understand why, despite how much money he was spending on Facebook ads, he wasn't making any money from his books. He was spending dozens of dollars a day and getting hundreds of clicks through to his product page on Amazon, but his sales weren't increasing.

One quick look at the Amazon product page for his book told me all I needed to know. Although his ad was great, the book cover looked like it had been designed in Microsoft Paint and the product description was bland and uninspiring.

He couldn't understand why people were clicking his ad and showing their interest in the book and then not buying it. I bit my tongue and tried to politely explain that the Amazon product page is your main shopfront, and that what's on there will make a reader decide whether to buy the book or not. It wasn't the ad he was trying to sell; it was the book.

As great as the ad looked, clickers were quickly presented with what looked like the very bottom of the pit of self-publishing circa 2009. It was no wonder he wasn't shifting any copies.

I explained that, rather than throw hundreds of dollars a week at non-converting Facebook ads, he should invest that same amount of money in a new, professionally designed cover and review his product description. He wouldn't even need to hire anyone to do the latter — I could see his sales copy was great from the text of his Facebook ad, which he wrote himself.

His response baffled me. He liked the cover, he told me. A friend of his had designed it based on a very specific brief he'd given her because he 'had a strong concept' of what it should look like. The fact that no-one else liked it and he was killing his career by using it didn't even seem to occur to him.

At least half a dozen times in my career, I've almost shelved a book I've been working on, convinced that it's dreadful. One of those books was *Her Last Tomorrow*, a book which I (thankfully) finished and released, only for it to earn me $150,000 in royalties in its first eight weeks on sale. It seems I have a very different taste in books to my readers!

And that's the key here. It would be disingenuous of me to tell you to ignore everything anyone else says and to plough on regardless, because your potential readers are the people who will transform your career one way or the other. If you're not giving readers what they want, you're not going to have a good time.

So what sort of things should you look out for?

AMAZON REVIEWS

I know. I know. I've said many, many times in interviews and in this book that I don't read Amazon reviews and that I don't recommend you do, either. Instead, I recommend asking a friend or family member (or, even better, hire a virtual assistant through a website such as Upwork) to have a browse through your Amazon reviews and look for common themes.

It might be that lots of readers comment on the fast pace of your books (good thing) or how much they are able to relate to the characters (good thing). It might even be that they didn't believe the character's motivations (bad thing) or thought the ending was rushed (bad thing).

By knowing the common things readers say about your books, you're not only getting valuable feedback but you're also distancing yourself from those comments. You don't have to read the exclamation-mark-laden vitriol that Barbara from Arizona wrote because you missed out a comma. But you do get to form a pretty good idea of what you're doing right and what you're doing wrong.

The key is not to listen to any one particular person. (I don't like *Star Wars*, but I'm well aware I'm in the minority here. Thank your lucky stars George Lucas didn't listen to *my* opinion.) By getting an overall picture of things, you'll get closer and closer to a true idea of what people think of your books.

This can be easily broken down into three steps:

1. Get someone without an emotional attachment to go through your reviews.
2. Ask them to jot down any common or repeated themes that crop up.
3. Do something about these (if negative) or use the positive ones to inform your marketing and promotions.

BUT I'M STILL WORKING ON MY FIRST BOOK!

Then you're in a beautiful virginal place where you don't have to worry about Amazon reviews. Yet. At some point your book will be finished and you'll be horribly defiled by someone you thought was going to love you forever but who still can't forgive you for that time you slipped on your keyboard in chapter five and called your main character Anddy.

If you're working on your first book, I'd highly recommend taking just two simple steps:

1. Finish the book.
2. Give it to an editor.

Find a good developmental editor and have them look at the book both from a structural and story point of view, as well as through the eyes of a reader. They provide incredible value for money, even if they seem expensive at the outset.

For authors who really aren't able to afford an editor from the outset (and, again, I must state my insistence that any viable business *needs* investment from its owner) you could use beta readers.

Beta readers are simply a small group of people who are representative of your readership (they could even be a small selection of your most ardent fans) who will happily read early versions of your work before it goes out into the wider world. They can help pick up on spelling, punctuation and grammar issues as well as any plot holes or character development errors which might negatively impact the book.

Imagine having a one-on-one writing coach who'll read your book, tell you how to improve it and set the foundations for the future success of your book. When you look at it that way, a developmental editor is a bargain.

These days I don't use developmental editors as such. The structure and recipe I've designed for my books is pretty tight, and I've learned how to master that side of things. But for your first book or two, a developmental editor will be invaluable.

So sit down, get that book finished and get a second (professional) pair of eyes on it.

HOW TO FIND AN EDITOR

There are lots of people who'll happily take your money in return for reading your book and moving a few apostrophes. These aren't editors. Editors will spend a long time reading and re-reading your book, examining its structure and plot development in order to help make your book the best it can be.

I recommend asking fellow authors for their recommendations with regards to editors (as long as their books are well edited and successful!). The Alliance of Independent Authors also has a Trusted Partners Directory on its website, which lists service providers whom they deem to be reputable and trustworthy. It can be found at: https://croft.link/ALLiTrustedPartners

DON'T ASK FAMILY AND FRIENDS

Please. Just don't. They'll always tell you your books are great, or they'll find ways to sugar coat it. Barbara from Arizona doesn't care. She won't hold back. If she hates it, she's going to say so.

Sure, the feedback from your family and friends

might be easier to take, but that's because they're *making* it easy. They don't want to hurt you. Barbara from Arizona, on the other hand, would hang you as soon as look at you.

Reviews from retailer websites are a great way to get this sort of impartial feedback, but there are other ways too. Why not try setting up a focus group? This can easily be done online using a secret group on Facebook or by finding readers in your local area.

Writing clubs can also be handy, but bear in mind that writers are often not the best judges of writing — see my earlier cautionary tale re: *Her Last Tomorrow*, which I nearly didn't finish. That's not the sort of break you want to miss out on. It's not other writers we want to please; it's readers.

The key here is that you should be prepared to listen to the opinions of people in general, but be careful not to hone in on the feedback from any one particular person. Yes, Barbara from Arizona. I'm looking at you.

SUMMARY POINTS

- **Understand your strengths and weaknesses.**

- Listen to those who are considered experts in their fields.
- Have someone analyse your Amazon reviews for common themes or constructive criticism.
- Ensure they also uncover what readers love about your books.
- Always use a professional editor where possible.
- Family and friends are lovely, but won't give you the feedback you need to develop your books.

WORKING WITH (OTHER) PROFESSIONALS

Knowing your limits is key. Do you think Jeff Bezos packs DVDs at the Amazon warehouses? Do you reckon Tim Cook hand-codes each new release of Safari?

These people know what they're good at, and they delegate the rest.

You're a writer. You're an entrepreneur. You are not a cover designer or an editor. Unless you are, in which case it's still **much** better to get an independent person to work on your books.

An independent professional can look at your book **objectively**. Think back to the author in the previous chapter who wanted my advice on why his book wasn't selling.

He loved his book's cover and product description, so he wasn't going to change them even though

I told him they were the reasons his book wasn't selling. He liked them, and that was that.

Of course, he's not the best judge of what would work best on his book. Neither am I, but at least I'm impartial and experienced. And that's the key.

Here's an example.

One of the hardest things for an author to do is to write their own book blurbs or product descriptions. We end up regurgitating the plot and telling the reader what happens.

Here's a little bit of advice for you: **the reader doesn't care what happens**.

She wants to know why she should buy and read the book. She'll find out what happens in her own good time. That's what the book is for. Your blurb or product description is your chance to hook potential readers and convince them to buy your book.

Bryan Cohen, one of the leading experts on blurbs and product descriptions, told me:

> When your book is listed on Amazon, it means that you have a sales page that you need to optimize. That's how any business online would look at it, and as an author entrepreneur, you need to do the same. Having a book description that is a subtle combination of mystery, marketing, and storytelling will help you to get more random browsers to click the buy button.
>
> When you send paid traffic to your book sales

page, the cover is often what gets people to the page. Your book description seals the deal. If you want to convert more strangers into potential fans, then getting the copywriting optimized for your book is essential. I recommend taking the time or spending the money necessary to give yourself the best chance of someone reading your description and adding your fantastic book to his or her device.

That's what any business person would do, and now that you're an author, you should do it too.

BRYAN COHEN

Bryan's *Best Page Forward* service is the sort of place you should be heading if you want a professionally written and optimised (sorry, Bryan — UK spellings here) product description or blurb.

But, whoever you use, the facts remain that writing blurbs and product descriptions is a highly skilled and specialist job in itself.

However, there are some fantastic books and resources for people who want to learn how to do this for themselves. I'd personally recommend:

Copyblogger.com/blog
A great free resource with regular tips and advice on copywriting in general.

How to Write a Sizzling Synopsis by **Bryan Cohen**
Written by one of the masters of book description copy, this is one of the only for-authors copywriting books on the market.

Copywriting Made Simple by **Tom Albrighton**
Although it's an all-encompassing book on writing promotional copy in general, Tom's book is generally considered to be one of the best copywriting books out there.

SUMMARY POINTS

- **Know the limits of your capabilities. And be honest with yourself about this.**
- **You're an author and entrepreneur — nothing else.**
- **Use objective, independent professionals where possible.**

OVERWHELM AND BURNOUT

OVERWHELM

This might be a familiar word for a few of you as you read this book.

A number of you will be feeling overwhelmed right now, particularly if you're a new writer or have realised that your previous mindset was a long way removed from the mindset you need to succeed as a writer.

That's fine. Honestly. It's perfectly natural.

I feel overwhelmed almost constantly. Right now I'm panicking about having to get this book finished, record the audio and form a marketing plan for it. Today I've realised I might have to set up a Facebook group for it or create some promotional videos.

It's a scorching hot day and I'm writing this on my laptop in my garden, which looks like a bomb's hit it. We've had a few days away at a wedding and funeral and I'm acutely aware I've got at least three days' work tidying up out here, and it's only going to get worse.

The house isn't much tidier, either. I feel like I'm constantly chasing my tail to keep it looking half-decent, which is difficult with two cats and a toddler running round the place.

I don't even have my next fiction book planned, and readers are already asking me when it's going to be released. I've not checked my AMS or BookBub ads in over a week. I've got a to-do list as long as my arm and almost a hundred unread emails in my inbox.

In short, I'm overwhelmed. You shouldn't feel ashamed if you are too. There are things that can be done.

DELEGATE

There's always someone else who can do it.

That goes for almost everything except one thing: writing your books.

No-one else can write with your voice and style, nor should they attempt to. Only you are you, and only you can write like you.

That said, you should focus on writing and leave everything else to someone else — even if only temporarily.

When I listed everything that was overwhelming me earlier, I had a closer look at what I actually *needed* to do and what could be delegated to someone else.

In terms of finishing this book, that has to be done by me. No questions. I consider the audiobook to be the same, as it would be bizarre for anyone else to read first-person non-fiction in my voice.

My garden's only going to get worse if I don't start on it soon, but my dad's a gardener. I can ask him for help.

The house is a no-brainer, too. After putting it into words a few moments ago, I took a short break, made a couple of phone calls and hired a cleaner. She starts next Wednesday.

Yes, I'm fortunate enough to be able to do that and I recognise many aren't. But we all have family or friends who'd be more than happy to help. You'd be amazed what people will do for you if you explain that you're struggling and really need their help.

If these things really need doing, who can you hire or ask to help you? We all get overwhelmed from time to time, and the person you ask for help will be no different. If you'd be willing to help them when you're less busy and they're struggling to keep their head above water, it could be a match made in heaven.

DON'T SWEAT THE SMALL STUFF

We all worry about things which don't need worrying about.

I mentioned earlier that I'm panicking about not having a Facebook group for this book and having not created any promotional videos.

So what?

No-one has asked for either of them. Literally no-one. They haven't even been mentioned as possibilities.

I've put all of that pressure on myself — entirely, and for no good reason.

Sure, a Facebook group and some promotional videos might help. Might. But what's the point in stressing about doing those before the book's even written? I can't promote something that doesn't exist.

Sometimes we all need to sit down, refocus and realign our priorities and realise what actually *needs* doing. Nine times out of ten, if you're a writer, the absolute number one priority is to write.

INFORMATION OVERLOAD

As an indie writer, you'll likely be overwhelmed by information. Everyone's an expert. Everyone's got an opinion.

This isn't a one-size-fits-all industry, which is just

another one of the reasons why this isn't a 'how to' book — there **isn't** a 'how to' that suits everyone.

It can be difficult to know what to read and who to listen to, especially when different people give you conflicting information. But there are two principles which have served me well, and which may well do the same for you.

LOOK WHO'S TALKING

Who's the expert? Is it someone who's sold millions of books, made loads of money and is considered to be someone who knows what they're talking about? Or is it someone you've never heard of, and who's not been *that* much more successful than you?

Looking at the source of the information is key to knowing who to trust and who to listen to. I'm not saying those who haven't made millions don't deserve your time and effort — far from it — but credentials are a valid and crucial filter when it comes to raising the signal:noise ratio in this industry.

TEST, TEST, TEST

There are very few facts in this industry. What works for you might not work for me, and vice versa.

The best thing you can do is to try things out, test

them and see what gives you results. Half of the fun of this industry is in the discovery, and testing allows you to do that every day.

The phrase 'your mileage may vary' is never truer than it is in this industry.

Sometimes, we work too hard. We take too much on. Put simply, we burn out.

We only have a finite amount of physical and mental energy, and if we try to use too much of it, we run into trouble.

That's why perspective is key.

PRIORITISING

List down everything that needs to be done, then look at each one in turn. Think about each one for a good minute or so. Does it **need** to be done? What will happen if you don't do it immediately? What will happen if you do it next week? What will happen if you never do it at all?

Putting things into perspective allows you to see

which tasks need doing now, and which ones can wait. That will take a lot of pressure off.

TAKE A BREAK

This might sound counterintuitive, but it works for both overwhelm and burnout.

When your mind isn't in the right place for taking on tasks, it needs to rest.

I regularly have days where I sit down at my desk to write in the morning and end up with ten or twelve words after half an hour. It just isn't happening. At that point, I have two choices.

I can either sit there for another half an hour and enjoy my twenty-five words, or I can go and do something else and let my brain relax.

Almost every time I do this, without fail, I sit back down and smash out a couple of thousand words.

The brain is a marvellous thing. It's well known that your mind will continue to work through a problem in the background, even whilst your conscious brain isn't aware of it. That's why the old adage says you should sleep on things that trouble you. Your brain will continue to work through it and, in the morning, you'll often have a fresh perspective and a clear answer.

Taking a bit of space away from the problem will help you in the long run. Just think about my own example. I take an hour out, then come back and write a thousand words in no time at all. If I stayed at my desk and wrote at my previous rate of ten words every half an hour, I'd have been at my desk for four days solid — with no sleep — to even get close to the same word count I had after an hour doing something else.

PART TWO

THE VISIONARY MINDSET

HOW TO BE A
VISIONARY

Stick with me. I'm not asking you to become the next Elon Musk.

Being a visionary is not about changing the world. It's about having the vision to look into the future and adapt your career and your business in preparation.

By now, I'm presuming you're in this for the long haul. You want writing to become your career and main source of income. And that's something that's a long-term plan and which will need to be sustained.

The visionary mindset is all about looking at the long-term. It's about understanding that instant results and long-term benefits are very different things and, often, mutually exclusive.

In the late 1960s and early 1970s, American psychologist Walter Mischel set up a number of studies at Stanford University on the subject of delayed gratification.

In the studies, children were put in a room and offered a small reward immediately, or a much larger reward if they waited a certain period of time.

Unsurprisingly, on the whole, the younger kids grabbed the treat (often a marshmallow) immediately, whereas the older, wiser kids waited it out and got more marshmallows at the end of the time period.

Of course, there were some younger kids who waited it out and some older ones who just couldn't help themselves.

But what was really astonishing was what happened to those kids afterwards. Subsequent studies showed there was a strong correlation between delayed gratification and future life success.

In short, the kids who realised they were better off waiting and getting more at a later date did far better in life (as measured by exam results, educational success, general health, salary earned and many other factors).

Let me hammer that home.

People who understand that it's better to take a small hit now for greater rewards later, do better in life.

And with that, let's begin.

SHORT TERM V LONG TERM THINKING

Unless you get *extremely* lucky, I can probably predict what's going to happen when you release your first (or next) book.

You'll get a small flurry of sales in the first day or two (almost without fail far fewer than you expected or hoped for), then it'll tail off and earn you a few dollars here and there. Sounds like a failure, right?

Wrong.

If you see that as a disappointment, you're yet to understand the power of residuals.

I have a lot of friends who are professional actors, and many of them have been appearing in films and TV shows for years. Even if they don't work for six months, they still earn money. Every time a TV show is repeated or someone buys a DVD of a film they were in, they (if their agent did their job properly) earn a royalty. Sure, it might only be a small amount of money here and there, but it's money for work they did *years* ago. That's a residual.

As well as books, I write plays. They're nowhere near as commercially successful as my books, but they earn some money. And I mean *some*. At the time of writing, the last royalty cheque I received from one of my play publishers was for £2.38. Still, that'll get me a packet of chocolate Hob Nobs and it's money for work I did three and a half years ago.

Many people call this 'sustainable' or 'passive' income. It's money you're making without doing any work. For more on this concept, I recommend listening to Pat Flynn's *Smart Passive Income* podcast.

It's the same for my books. At the time of writing, one of my poorest selling books, *Guilty as Sin*, made £6 on Amazon Kindle yesterday. That's a pretty typical day for that book. It was the second book I ever wrote, back in 2011 — seven years ago.

That book earns £6 a day **every day**. That's £180 a month, or £2,160 a year. That might not sound a lot, but that's a very nice holiday every year, effectively free, for work I did seven years ago. When you consider that's one of my weakest-selling books (and only one of twenty-odd titles I have on sale), you can start to imagine how quickly it adds up. Even if *all* my books only made £6 a day each, I'd be looking at over £4,000 a month in Kindle royalties alone. Even if

I only had ten books on sale, I'm looking at making the average UK wage (around £25,000/$35,000) purely through work I've already done.

When I include all my titles, so far this year (it's June as I write this) I've had four months out of six in which I've earned more than £40,000, with royalties totalling just over £216,000 between January and June. That's the power of residuals.

Excited now? Good. You should be. Because this concept is at the heart of the indie author mindset that you need to key into.

When the *20 Books to 50k* craze hit a couple of years back, it seemed to revolutionise many authors' outlooks on their own writing.

In short, *20 Books* states that once you've written twenty titles and marketed them effectively, that backlist of books will enable you to sustain a $50,000 income. In short, that's because each book only needs to earn you $2,500 a year (or just over $200 a month, or $7 a day).

Many authors in the early stages of their career will see $200 a month or $7 a day as very achievable targets. And that's because they are. It's the compounding of that multiple across twenty books which makes it so powerful. This is residuals in action.

Do the sums. If each of your books made $7 a day, how many books would you need to have out to replace your current salary?

20 Books to 50k is nothing new. It didn't blow me away when it hit the scene because it was something I already knew and which seemed as natural as breathing air rather than water. Build a library of products and you're set for life. Simple. But to many people it was revolutionary. For those who *didn't* have a business mindset, *20 Books* was a very well described concept which enabled them to see the light.

Whichever way works for you, the important thing is that you shift your way of thinking, because the business mindset is absolutely crucial to your success as an author.

As a close to this chapter, and now that you understand the power of residuals and having a back catalogue of books, you need to sit down and look at how many books you've written to date. How many are on sale? If it's fewer than five, I'd strongly advise you to put this book down, write more books and get them ready for publication. Building your catalogue of books is, by far, the most crucial, simple action you can take to revolutionise and future-proof your indie author career.

Woah! He just called writing a load more books 'simple'!

Well, yeah. I did. If you're reading this book, it's because you already *are* a writer. You've likely written a book or are partway through doing so. You already know how to write books. Writing more *is* the simplest thing you'll have to do in your career.

SUMMARY POINTS

- One book doesn't need to be a runaway success — a few dollars a day soon adds up.
- This effect can be compounded by writing more books.
- Long-term thinking is crucial to your indie author career. A larger catalogue of books will provide future-proofing.
- WRITE MORE BOOKS.

There are a lot of practicalities to consider when you're an indie author. But if you keep the concept of ownership in mind, you won't go far wrong.

Ownership is about far more than intellectual property, but that does form a large part of it. It's more about control and future development.

Having complete control over everything you do is probably one of the main reasons you decided to go indie in the first place, so why would you relinquish that?

When you're just starting out as an author, it can be tempting to cut corners and try to save costs, but you could be shooting yourself in the foot in the long-term.

Where possible, ensure you've got complete control and ownership. There are a few places in which new authors tend to fall over here:

YOUR AUTHOR WEBSITE

It can be really tempting to set up a website for free at Wix, Weebly or Wordpress.com (why do these things always begin with W?)

It's quick, it's easy and it's free. What's not to love, right?

It's also pretty unprofessional and disrespectful to your own career. You're asking people to part with their hard-earned money, but you won't part with your own to invest in your own products and storefront.

I highly recommend Wordpress, but please, *please* use it on a self-hosted platform. These are often remarkably cheap. Big names like GoDaddy offer Wordpress hosting from just $3.99 a month. My own recommended web host, Siteground, starts from just $3.95.

If your author website is your main storefront, why give effective control to a third-party? Keep your website and your vital tools under your own control.

ISBNS

CreateSpace offer you a free ISBN when you publish a paperback through them, so why not use it?

The same principles apply. Besides which, the book will look quite obviously self-published on the

Amazon product page with CreateSpace listed as the publisher. This can put readers off. If your aim is to make your books indistinguishable from traditionally published books (and it *should* be), why cut corners?

The eagle-eyed amongst you might have noticed that some of my books have CreateSpace ISBNs. Remember that bit earlier where I mentioned I made a lot of mistakes in my early years in publishing? Yeah. That. I'm working on it.

ISBNs aren't cheap, but get a lot cheaper if you buy more. I bought a block of 100 ISBNs from Nielsen (the UK registrar), mainly to make it cheaper per-unit and to force myself to write 100 books.

ISBNs future-proof your books. Although Amazon assign an ASIN to your book and all the other vendors will give it some sort of product identifier, what happens when those vendors no longer exist? Many are already seeing their market share squeezed, and NOOK now only operates in the US. What if Amazon moves away from ASIN? Your ISBN is permanent and will always be owned by you.

There are also some sticky legal aspects behind ISBNs. If you don't own the ISBN, it's arguable that you aren't technically the publisher. The owner of the book's ISBN is. Do you really want someone else having that control over your books?

Ownership of your data and intellectual copyright is something I'm passionate about, as is having complete control over your career.

On which note…

SUMMARY POINTS

- **Ensure you maintain control in all areas where possible.**
- **Set up a self-hosted website.**
- **Buy and use your own ISBNs.**

CONTROL IN DISTRIBUTION AND MARKETING

This is a debate which has raged in the indie author community for years, and it's not about to stop.

Put simply, when referring to the availability of their books, indie authors can be two things: **wide or exclusive**.

This has only really become a talking point since Amazon introduced KDP Select as a publishing option. Select gives authors a (diminishing) number of benefits, the principle of which is the ability to have your books included in Kindle Unlimited.

Kindle Unlimited (KU) is a subscription service which allows readers to pay a few dollars a month and "borrow" and read as many books as they like throughout that month. (Technically, only ten books at a time can be borrowed, but that's only ever an issue if you've actually got ten books on the go at once.)

The catch is that to have your books included in Kindle Unlimited, they must be absolutely exclusive to Amazon.

For those who haven't quite cottoned on, that means you can't sell digital copies of your books anywhere else except through Amazon Kindle. In return, authors are paid for the number of pages of their books that are read.

This works for many authors. Some genres, such as romance, Young Adult and erotica are practically designed for KU — their readers devour books, often reading many in a week, and the cut-price subscription service is absolutely ideal for them.

However, there are some significant drawbacks.

AUTONOMY

For me, this is the biggie. Trust me, I've been locked into contracts with Amazon for longer than I care to remember, and it's not fun.

Two of my books were published by their crime and thriller imprint, Thomas & Mercer, and the lack of freedom and autonomy I'd enjoyed as an indie author was excruciating. Fortunately, I managed to get out of that contract and all my books are now owned exclusively by me.

If all your eggs are in Amazon's basket, you may as well be traditionally published and have your books in major bookstores, too. That's great if you're willing to lose your autonomy and sleep at night hoping you don't wake up to find your KDP account shut down for no reason at all (this happens to dozens of authors a week, when Amazon's bots and algorithms decide they think you've done something wrong). Alternatively, Amazon could either decide to stop selling ebooks or go bust altogether. I know, I know, but stranger things have happened. No company lasts forever. Every most-successful-company-in-the-world has collapsed.

Look at Compaq Computers. In the 1990s they were the number one seller of IBM personal computers. They now no longer exist.

Kodak, the world leader in photographic equipment, went bankrupt in 2012.

General Motors was the world's leading manufacturer of vehicles for 77 years. In 2009, GM filed for bankruptcy.

Lehman Brothers was one of the world's biggest investment banks. It filed for bankruptcy in 2008, taking many of the world's economies down with it, leaving entire countries in billions of dollars of debt.

Disruption is the only constant in life. Amazon itself was a disruption to the physical retail shopping economy and revolutionised the way people read and, eventually, something will happen to disrupt it too. Is it a risk worth taking?

LOSS OF SALES ELSEWHERE

If you go all-in with Amazon, you *won't* sell any books at Kobo, Apple iBooks, Google Play or Barnes & Noble NOOK — because you won't be allowed to.

Personally, I sell a lot of books on all of those platforms, and I've had whole months in which Amazon wasn't even my most lucrative distributor. Amazon's share is dwindling for me, so it makes no sense to keep my books exclusive to them.

CLOSED ECOSYSTEM

If your books are only available on Amazon, there are millions of readers who will never read your books. Lots of people don't have Kindles or won't shop at Amazon.

Amazon is only the biggest ebook retailer in the UK, US and a small handful of other countries. In both Canada and Australia, for example, Amazon lags behind. And both of those countries are huge markets.

Kobo is the market leader in Canada, is second in the UK and is growing exponentially in Australia.

Apple iBooks is also growing in much of the world, although they're frustratingly slow to capitalise on their enormous potential and I feel will probably never become an industry leader in ebooks.

Google Play is growing across the world, and

especially in emerging markets where lower-priced Android devices are starting to flood the market. I enjoy significant and growing sales at Google Play each month, despite doing absolutely no marketing there whatsoever.

Barnes & Noble NOOK, despite being a great platform and having some wonderful people working there, has suffered declining market share for years, and now only operates in the United States, where its only option is to try and take on the Amazon behemoth. I sincerely hope it succeeds, but I do worry for it. Having said that, I've recently had months where I've made over $6,000 at NOOK.

POLITICS

It's got to be said: lots of people just don't like Amazon. For whatever reasons, a lot of people are opposed to the way they do things and just won't deal with them. For me, that's an opinion that must be respected. Apart from that, you're leaving money on the table by ignoring those readers just because of their political principles.

The argument can easily be broken down into a list of pros and cons, at which point the balance of power seems pretty clear:

KDP SELECT

Advantages

- Income from Kindle Unlimited pot based on page reads
- Access to some promotional tools such as Kindle Countdown deals

Disadvantages

- Can only sell books via Amazon
- No sales from other platforms
- Reliant on one company for all your income
- Risk of Amazon pulling the plug on your livelihood

WIDE DISTRIBUTION

Advantages

- Sell your books through any platform or distributor you choose
- Ensure that all potential readers are able to access and buy your books

- No reliance on one single company for all your income
- No risk of Amazon pulling the plug on your livelihood

Disadvantages

- No access to Kindle Countdown deals
- No share of the Kindle Unlimited pot
- Continual marketing required to perform well on other platforms

You've probably noticed by now that you're not going to get a completely impartial overview of the wide/exclusive debate from me. I come down on the wide side of things in almost every aspect of the argument, and I wouldn't change that for the world. I know there'll be a significant number of you reading this who'll be frothing at the mouth at my insistence that being wide is best for all authors. But I honestly believe that is true.

If anyone asks me my opinion on whether they should be wide or exclusive, I always advise being wide, and you will have far more opportunities afforded to you that way and far fewer sleepless nights, but ultimately it's a decision that must be yours.

For new authors, though, there really is no harm in trying KDP Select. My books are the income for my entire family. If you're at the start of your career, your situation is likely to be rather different.

Only having one dashboard and one distributor to focus on is, undeniably, much easier but it's not a realistic, ambitious or safe long-term business plan for me.

Perhaps it's a matter of genre. Romance authors, for example, should almost certainly consider KDP Select very strongly.

Romance readers consume books voraciously. Those guys simply can't afford to buy each book individually. Kindle Unlimited is a godsend for them, and as an author you'd be verging on crazy to ignore that market. The same goes for Young Adult fiction.

If you write crime, thrillers, sci-fi or fantasy, putting the effort into going wide and marketing your books on other platforms will likely reap big rewards.

It's also worth noting that KDP Select's enrolment periods are based on a three-month rolling contract. You're free to dip in and out every three months, but people who have done so report that this can harm sales and rankings.

If you're still not convinced, why not give KDP Select a go? There are lots of authors who make considerably more money than me, and solely through KDP Select. Personally, that reliance on and trust in Amazon just isn't there for me, so I wouldn't take that risk, but I can understand those who do.

SUMMARY POINTS

- Understand the advantages and disadvantages of being exclusive and wide.
- KDP Select can be useful for authors at the start of their career.
- For a truly long-term, scalable business plan, I strongly advise going wide.

'Wide' is a vague term. It basically means 'not just Amazon', but you might be surprised at exactly what that encompasses.

At the time of writing, there are more than sixty ebook distributors and platforms from which readers can buy books. Quite honestly, I have no idea why. There are essentially only two ebook formats worth bothering with: MOBI and ePUB. MOBI is Amazon's format and everyone else uses ePUB.

One of the principles I adhere to a lot, and which you should ask yourself right now is: Is the juice worth the squeeze?

Uploading a book to each of these 60+ distributors would take you days, possibly longer. And that'll have to be done every time you write a new book or make a change to an existing one (which might just be as simple as tweaking a price for a one-day promotion). However, there are other options:

USE AN AGGREGATOR

I won't go into the details here, as they're for another book, but aggregators will take your book and push it out to a number of different distributors. As far as you're concerned, you have one dashboard, one entry point and lots of sales outlets. The disadvantages are that the aggregator takes a cut of your earnings and you won't have direct contact with the distributors or retailers.

The two main aggregators at the time of writing are Draft2Digital and Smashwords, who will push your books out to the main ebook retailers and also deal with library distribution of ebooks.

GO DIRECT TO THE BIG PLAYERS

This is the option I use and advocate for a couple of reasons. First of all, it ensures your books are on all the big platforms. At the time of writing, they're Amazon Kindle, Kobo, Apple iBooks, Google Play and Barnes & Noble NOOK. It also means you get all the royalties due to you, can set up promotions directly with the retailers and aren't beholden to one aggregator who could disappear or close your account down.

Going direct is much easier these days than it was. Many people still think iBooks and Kobo are difficult to get set up on. They aren't. Things have changed massively, and I personally find the aggregators clunkier and more difficult to work with.

Retailers such as Tolino, Scribd and Playster have their place, but in my experience aren't worth the time and effort of publishing with them. Your mileage may vary, of course.

SUMMARY POINTS

- **Aggregators are a handy, low-effort way of getting your books to market on all vendors.**
- **You can earn more money and get more promotional opportunities by going direct to the retailers.**

THE POWER OF A MAILING LIST

Your mailing list will form the core of your marketing plan and the bedrock for your future success. This, perhaps more than any other form of marketing, requires a massive shift in mindset.

WHAT IS A MAILING LIST?

A mailing list is a list of people who've expressed their interest in your books, and who've given you their permission to email them.

From time to time, you can use your email marketing software to engage with your subscribers and keep them up to date with your latest news, including new book releases.

WHY ARE MAILING LISTS SO IMPORTANT?

I've spoken about autonomy a few times already. Keeping control over your assets and ensuring that you're beholden to no-one else is incredibly important.

If you were in any other business selling any other product, you'd probably know who every one of your customers was. You'd get their names and addresses every time they bought from you and you'd be able to call them up and speak to them. You'd have all sorts of data, far beyond the raw number of units you've sold and the money you've earned.

Amazon knows exactly who buys what products, with what frequency and how they shop in general. That's how they manage to suggest just the right products at just the right time. They know who buys certain types of books, and they suggest other books they might like to read too.

In conjunction with Facebook (and a piece of code called a pixel), companies can access browsing behaviours. Facebook knows when you've got a new baby, because you put the pictures up or talk about the lack of sleep. It knows how old you are, whether you're married and what car you drive. And advertisers can use this data to laser-target you with their products.

In short, all smart businesses use customer data to drive future sales. It's an extremely effective business tool and one which is crucial to survival in the modern marketplace.

However, as an indie author, all that data is owned by Amazon, Kobo, Apple and the other retailers. They know exactly who's buying your books, but they're not about to tell you. That's why you need to get control over your data.

BENEFITS OF A MAILING LIST

Mailing lists are very inexpensive (and can be free if you don't have many subscribers) and they allow you to keep in touch with your readers and let them know when you've got a new book out. Just imagine the sheer power behind being able to send an email to your readers telling them your new book is ready for them to buy — and it won't cost you a penny. It's a direct route, and is essentially a free or very inexpensive form of marketing.

Email marketing works. Readers open the emails and act on the content inside. Again, this is a whole subject for another book, but for now think of it as building your customer database.

GETTING THE DATA

Before GDPR data regulations came into effect in 2018, this was much easier. Savvy authors used to put a message in the front and back of their books offering a free book or bonus content, which'd be emailed to them if they entered their email address in a form.

This can still be done, but needs to be framed differently. The newsletter (mailing list) signup needs to be front and centre, with the bonus content or free book framed as an added extra. It's not only important that users consent to being on your mailing list: it's the law.

Nowadays, mass signups through giveaways aren't as common, but the value of the readers signing up has increased as a result. Rather than simple freebie-chasers joining your list, you'll be getting engaged readers who genuinely want to hear from you.

ENGAGING WITH YOUR READERS

I could fill a whole book on this subject, but there are some basic principles which I think all authors can apply to the way they deal with their mailing list:

GET IN TOUCH FREQUENTLY

Most email marketing experts agree that about once a week is optimal. Any more than that and you risk being seen as too keen; any less and they'll forget who you are. At a minimum, you should aim for once a fortnight. Readers read lots of books by lots of authors, and they won't remember you or how much they loved your books unless you keep in touch.

There's an old adage in marketing known as The Rule of Seven, which dictates that — on average — a potential customer needs to see or hear about your company or product seven times before they'll consider buying it. This is where your earlier branding work will lay down the foundations for that future sale.

ENGAGE ON A PERSONAL LEVEL

I not only use my mailing list to let readers know when I've got a new book out, but I also give them snippets about my life. Nothing too personal, but things they might find interesting. I recently took part in a charity run, so I shared it with them. Last year I visited a local prison to give a talk, so I shared that with them. The email which had the most responses (over 1,500) was when I told them my son had been born. And yes, I replied to every single one. Which reminds me…

ENGAGE FOR THE LONG-TERM

If a reader replies to your email marketing or otherwise gets in touch, engage them in conversation. Thank them for their kind words, at the very least. Readers will often see you as some form of celebrity for having written a book, and it'll quite likely make their day that you took the time to respond. This is a key part of getting them to become a super-fan (or 'brand advocate').

I spoke to David Gaughran, the author of *Strangers to Superfans*, about the importance of email marketing and engaging with your readers.

He told me:

Email is the most powerful tool that any author has at their disposal. Having a big list will add serious power to every launch and promotion you run. Not only that, email also gives you an opportunity to turn purchasers into true fans—the kind of passionate advocates for your work who do the selling for you. Sounds good, right?

Problem is, writers often focus on the first thing (getting a big list) and don't put much effort in to the second (creating superfans via engagement), which should be your true aim. Rather than chasing numbers, treat each name on your list as a person and seek to create a community. Instead of only mailing people when you want something -

and yes, a new release is still an "ask" because you want their money - try and create value for your readers in every email you send, and make sure that you keep in touch with them regularly.

Turning readers into passionate fans requires that engagement I mentioned, and email is by far the best tool for the job. And the cool thing is this: if you focus on creating happy, engaged subscribers, then all that other stuff you are chasing - numbers, sales, rank, money - falls into place anyway, and in a much more sustainable way.

DAVID GAUGHRAN

THINKING AHEAD (DIRECT SALES)

Imagine a time when Amazon doesn't exist. It'll happen. That's almost guaranteed. Every company that's ever existed will close down at some point in time. And what will you do then? Sure, you could use the other ebook retailers who'll take up the slack and become the new big players. But you'll have to start your marketing from scratch.

Readers read tons of authors. They'll remember maybe a small handful of their names. The onus is on *you* to keep in touch with *them*.

Even if Amazon will be around for a while yet, direct ebook sales are becoming big business. Lots of authors are selling books directly from their website using services such as BookFunnel plugged into PayPal, giving authors an effective 97% royalty on each book they sell.

I've experimented with this model in the past, and it works well. There are advantages and disadvantages, but if this becomes a credible and popular way forward for authors and readers, you'll have a head start by being able to send your readers directly to the sales page on your website.

Bear in mind that you'll only be able to do this if you're wide. Selling books from your own website is a direct violation of Amazon's Terms of Service if you're in KDP Select.

This, for me, is another huge reason not to be in KDP Select. Selling direct through your website has become so lauded in recent times that a whole new phase of the industry has been heralded and named 'Self Publishing 3.0'.

It isn't something I think is ever going to be a credible or majority market at any point in the future, but it is a sensible and mature contingency plan which backs up my message on ownership and control.

HOW TO START YOUR MAILING LIST

I won't go too heavily into how to set up your mailing list, but I will give you a brief overview of the major players so you can decide which mailing list provider might be best for you.

MAILCHIMP

Simple to use, free if you have fewer than 2,000 subscribers. Advanced 'power' features are available for a subscription fee. Paid-for plans are more expensive than some other platforms, and open rates can vary.

MAILERLITE

I have used MailerLite in the past, but no long recommend doing so. They've had some well-publicised issues with spam traps and anecdotal evidence shows that open rates are much lower than with other providers. In 2017, EmailToolTester.com conducted a range of studies and declared MailerLite to have one of the worst deliverability results in the industry, with just 77.64% of emails reaching their destination. MailChimp scored 87.52%, Constant Contact 89.74% and ConvertKit 92.1%. In the same study, not a single email sent by MailerLite to an Outlook or Hotmail address reached a user's inbox.

AWEBER, INFUSIONSOFT, CONVERTKIT & CONSTANT CONTACT

These are both far more powerful email marketing platforms, but I must admit that I've never found any use for their extra bells and whistles. My email marketing uses are fairly advanced, especially compared to most authors, and MailChimp has never let me down in that regard.

BACKING UP

Whichever mailing list provider you choose to use, please make sure you backup your list regularly — I suggest weekly.

Most of the providers allow you to export your list as a CSV file, which will protect you if the provider loses your data or — God forbid — disappears overnight.

However you store this data, you must make sure it's within the guidance of GDPR and other data protection regulations.

SUMMARY POINTS

- **Your mailing list is the core of everything you do from a marketing point of view.**
- **Ownership of your customer data is key.**

- Ensure you comply with GDPR data regulations at all times.
- Engage with your readers frequently, on a personal level and for the long-term.
- Take a look at the main email marketing providers to see which suits you best.
- Backup your mailing list regularly (at least weekly).

As an indie author you're completely in control of your own destiny, right? To an extent, yes. But we are all still reliant on Amazon, Apple, Kobo, Google and all the other platforms to uphold their side of the bargain.

And by the time you're ready to negotiate for foreign rights or even film and TV deals, you're going to need help. Agents can be great for this, but will want to take a substantial cut of your earnings in return.

If you haven't got foreign publishers or film and TV companies approaching you, an agent can also help build some interest around your books. They'll tout them to producers and foreign publishers and try to seek deals on your behalf.

Agents will not charge a fee for their services, but

will instead take a cut of any deals they manage to complete for you. 10-20% is fairly standard, depending on what's being negotiated. An agent who asks for a retainer or upfront fees should be avoided.

On the other hand, if you've got offers coming out of your ears, you're the one in control and you can choose how you negotiate the terms.

I would not advise you to do this yourself. I can't say that any more strongly, so please just take my word for it. Even if you 'used to deal with contracts' in your old job or 'have a cousin who's a solicitor', this area of law is extremely specialist and unless that cousin is a contracts lawyer for a literary agency with a film and TV arm, I'd highly recommend you do things properly.

There are a number of ways in which you can get screwed over with translation and media rights contracts, and even a fully-qualified solicitor might not spot many of them unless they're a specialist in this precise area of law.

Fortunately, you don't need to pay for a specialist lawyer to do this for you. Not directly, anyway.

There are two extremely useful organisations which all indie authors should join: the Society of Authors and the Alliance of Independent Authors.

SOCIETY OF AUTHORS

The Society of Authors (SoA) has been in existence since 1884 and counts such literary giants as Alfred Lord Tennyson, George Bernard Shaw, E. M. Forster, J. M. Barrie, Thomas Hardy and H. G. Wells amongst its former members and presidents.

In the UK, the SoA is the most prominent trade union for authors, and it does a huge amount of campaigning on their behalf. The SoA bangs the drum for ensuring authors are fairly paid for speaking engagements, pushes for audits on publishers and generally fights for authors' rights.

For your £102 a year (at the time of writing) you also get access to the Society's specialist contract lawyers. This is extremely useful, as hiring a specialist lawyer to look over a contract for you would likely cost a lot more than this, especially if revisions are required.

Self-published authors are, contrary to popular belief, perfectly eligible to join the Society of Authors as Full Members. The only requirement is that they've sold over 300 print copies or 500 ebooks in twelve months. That equates to 25 print copies or 42 ebooks a month — not an unreasonable target even for an author at the start of their career. If you are yet to reach that target, you can join the Society as an Associate Member.

Membership is available worldwide.

More information is available at societyofauthors.org

ALLIANCE OF INDEPENDENT AUTHORS

The Alliance of Independent Authors (ALLi) was set up by a group of Society of Authors members in the days before the Society admitted independently published authors.

Like the Society, it does a lot of fantastic work in banging the drum for indie authors and ensuring that they are fairly represented. It runs the Indie Author Fringe to accompany various large book fairs and has a very successful presence at many other events throughout the calendar year.

It offers three levels of membership: Associate for authors who haven't yet published their book, Author for writers who've published their work and Professional for authors who've sold more than 50,000 copies of their books. Subscription rates are £55, £75 and £99 a year respectively.

Membership is available worldwide.

More information is available at croft.link/ALLi

SUMMARY POINTS

- Consider engaging a film & TV or foreign rights agent.
- Use the services of the Society of Authors and the Alliance of Independent Authors to help you negotiate contracts.

PART THREE

THE BUSINESS MINDSET

INTRODUCTION

Not having a business mindset held me back in my career for years. There have been many times since, where not applying the business mindset would have made everything fall apart. The business mindset is **crucial** to your success as an independent author. You are:

- an author
- a publisher
- a businessperson.

The three are inseparable, and with very good reason.

Although I've run small businesses in the past, it took me a long time to realise that those business principles I'd learned over the years could — and should — be applied to my writing career. When I applied those principles, everything changed.

I started to market and advertise my books. I began to learn what worked and didn't work in marketing them. I realised very quickly that there are a LOT of books out there and that I needed to grab potential readers' attention quickly. That's when I figured out that completing and marketing that unfinished book in my drawer could be a game changer.

That book was called *Her Last Tomorrow* and carries the hook 'Could you murder your wife to save your daughter?'

The book responded very well to marketing via Facebook Ads. Within a day or two the book was doubling (sometimes trebling) whatever I was spending on the ads. My business mindset told me I had to spend more. After all, if I'm doubling whatever I'm spending, why would I not want to spend whatever I could?

I slowly ramped up the spend to the point where I was spending £1,000 a day on the ads. I didn't have £1,000 a day, but I did have a few things: friends, family, credit cards and **solid data**. This last item is emboldened for a reason. We'll come back to it later in the book.

It's important to note that this is *not* about budget. The same principle applied at £5 a day and £1,000 a day. In fact, it applied *more* at £5 a day, and was the reason *why* I ramped it up as far as I did. The physical numbers are irrelevant; it's the principle and the theory that matters, and the savvy author ignores it at her peril.

I could see by tracking my sales exactly how much I was earning in royalties every day, and Facebook was telling me exactly what I was spending on ads on those same days. Every time I ramped it up, I made double the spend in book royalties.

Now, most people would poop their pants long before £1,000 a day. If I wasn't applying my business mindset, I might've done the same. But that would have made absolutely no sense. I'd still be spending £10 a day and making £20 a day, instead of spending £1,000 a day and making £2,000 a day. I know which I'd rather have.

The problem was that Facebook took my money for the ads that same day, and Amazon took anything up to 60 days to pay me my royalties. That left a cashflow shortfall of about £60,000 which I needed to pay for the ads before the royalties came in.

I grabbed every credit card I had to my name and found my credit limits came to £15,000. I went online and applied for as many more as I could, and managed to up my credit to £40,000. At that point I went to family and friends, showed them the data I had in my spreadsheets and asked them if they'd lend me the remaining money. Because I had the right business mindset and solid data, they agreed.

I also knew that I could see *instantaneously* how much I was spending on ads and what I was making in book sales. The moment the latter failed to exceed the former, I could flick a button, switch the lot off and take the money thankyouverymuch. But it carried on doubling my money, and I certainly wasn't complaining.

The success of that book changed my life. If I hadn't had the business mindset to look at the data, see what was happening and understand the logic in upping my advertising spend as much as possible, I'd still be earning £20 a day.

As an independent author, you are producing and selling a product, and that is no different to any other business producing and selling any other product. The same principles apply, and they're not difficult ones to master.

SUMMARY POINTS

- **You are a businessperson.**
- **Trust the data.**
- **Invest and increase spending on things that turn a profit in order to maximise those profits.**

LET'S INCORPORATE

One of the first things I did when I started writing was to incorporate it into a proper, bona fide business.

The advantages of doing this are numerous. Depending on the country you're in there are probably tax advantages, but that's a subject for far more qualified people than me.

What I'm interested in is mindset.

There are two ways in which people approach the business side of things. If you paid attention in Part I, you'll probably know what they are already.

THE HOBBYIST

The hobbyist is quite happy to have his book royalties paid into his personal account. It's a nice bit of extra money on top of his salary.

He is the writer, and he gets to enjoy the fruits of those labours. To him, writing is a personal thing.

THE PROFESSIONAL

The professional has incorporated her company and has a separate business bank account. To her, this is an official venture. She means business.

She separates herself from the writing, understanding her books are a product which generate the money she needs to write more and enjoy life.

No prizes for guessing which one of the two is likely to be the most successful.

Being registered as a business is more than just 'making it official', though. It's about separation of identity.

In *The War of Art*, Steven Pressfield describes this beautifully:

> I like the idea of being Myself, Inc. That way I can wear two hats. I can hire myself and fire myself.
>
> STEVEN PRESSFIELD - THE WAR OF ART

In the UK, at least, forming a limited company means that you are legally separate from the business. The company employs you. You are not the company.

This is a subtle but crucial difference which goes far, far beyond legalities and definition.

As the owner of a business, you're in charge of its performance. You can kick yourself up the arse when things aren't going well. You're responsible for the success.

As the writer, you're an employee of the business. It's your writing that enables the company to make money. You're answerable to the other you — the boss.

> If we think of ourselves as a corporation, it gives us a healthy distance on ourselves. We're less subjective. We don't take blows as personally. We're more cold-blooded; we can price our wares more realistically. Sometimes, as Joe Blow himself, I'm too mild-mannered to go out and sell. But as Joe Blow, Inc., I can pimp the hell out of myself. I'm not me anymore. I'm Me, Inc.
>
> STEVEN PRESSFIELD, THE WAR OF ART

Rules, regulations and procedures vary across the world. For more information on incorporating as a company, I recommend you speak to an accountant or business advisor in your country.

SUMMARY POINTS

- **Go from hobbyist to professional by setting up as an official company.**
- **Incorporating separates you from your business and allows you to look at it objectively.**

MONEY

MONEY IS NOT EVIL

I'm conflicted when it comes to business. My moral compass points firmly away from money, but the fact of the matter is that we all need it. Money rules everything we do, whether we like it or not (and I don't much).

And let's face it: if money didn't matter, you wouldn't be reading this book. You'd be content just writing your books and putting them out there, or you would've given your life savings to one of those scam artists we talked about earlier. Presumably (unless you've got really lost) you're here because you want to earn at least enough money out of your writing to be able to write more.

There's nothing wrong with wanting to sell more books. There's nothing wrong with wanting to provide for your family, take them on nice holidays and let them drive around in nice cars. That needn't be at odds with the 'money is evil' mindset that so many of us creatives have.

At the very least, put it this way: earning money from your writing will allow you to invest more money in marketing and advertising your books, opening them up to a wider audience.

That's something I suggest all authors do, in fact. The ratios will be different for different authors based on their individual genre and profit margin, but a decent percentage of what you earn from your writing should be put straight back into marketing and advertising. More on that later.

SUMMARY POINTS

- **It's fine to want to make money.**
- **Accept that earning good money from your writing will give you the freedom to write more.**

The concept of profit is a remarkably simple one to explain:

$$\text{Income (I) - Expenditure (E) = Profit (P)}$$

- **Income** is money that comes into your bank account from your book sales
- **Expenditure** is what you spend on trying to get those sales
- **Profit** is the difference between the two.

Just so I look really intelligent, let's call it P=I-E. I was going to throw in a couple of square roots and the infinity sign to make myself look even more clever, but then it wouldn't have spelt 'pie'.

In all seriousness, though, it's quite literally as easy as P=I-E.

If you spend a hundred dollars in a month and you bring in five hundred dollars, you've made a profit of four hundred dollars.

TURNOVER

Turnover is the amount of money your business has coming in. It's also called income or revenue.

From a business point of view, in terms of gauging success, this should largely be ignored. Lots of companies and people will boast about how they or their company 'turned over' a million dollars last year. Sounds great, right? Not if they spent two million, it isn't. As all good pie lovers know, that means you've lost a million dollars. That puts you approximately a million dollars worse off than a homeless person on the streets. In the words of Shania Twain, That Don't Impress Me Much.

Ask yourself this, using your new knowledge of pie: Would you rather turn over a thousand dollars with a profit of five hundred dollars, or turnover a thousand dollars with a loss of five hundred?

Personally, I'd rather make five hundred dollars than lose five hundred.

RETURN ON INVESTMENT

Return on investment (ROI) is really just a funky way of measuring direct profit. This is something I'll skim over here, because it's a subject for a whole other book on more advanced marketing techniques, but it can be summarised thus:

$$ROI = Profit / Expenditure$$

ROI is always expressed as a percentage, and can be further expanded to include the profit calculation:

$$ROI = (Income - Expenditure) / Expenditure$$

So, let's say for argument's sake that I spend $100 on Facebook ads and those ads directly generate $200 in sales. Following the formula:

$$(\$200 - \$100) / \$100$$

gives you an ROI of 1. Expressed as a percentage, this is 100%, meaning you've doubled your money (something you could've worked out more quickly by looking at the income and expenditure in the first place).

But when the numbers get a bit funkier, ROI is a great way of comparing different days, weeks, months or advertising media in order to gauge success.

Let's say I spend $71.76 on ads and make $322.93 in revenue (income). Following the ROI formula, the answer is a shade over 3.5, or 350% when expressed as a percentage.

A loss would be expressed as a minus percentage, e.g. -350%.

Want to get back to some more fun stuff? Sure. Let's do it. But first, we need to take another stepping stone that focuses on money — although in a far less scientific, more philosophical way.

SUMMARY POINTS

- Understand income, expenditure and profit. They're far simpler than people make out.
- Turnover is an irrelevance at this stage. What matters is whether you're making or losing money.
- Understand return on investment (ROI).

A lot of authors who come to me for help and assistance seem to have real difficulty grasping the difference between an expense and an investment.

The two are very closely linked, and many dictionary definitions explain expenses or costs in a way which makes them sound like investments, but there is one crucial difference — and it's one which could transform your career.

Earlier in this section I told you my story about how my life changed when my book *Her Last Tomorrow* started responding remarkably well to Facebook ads. I told you I ended up spending as much money as I could, purely because every pound I spent was being doubled. Instead of doubling £10 a day, I started doubling £1,000 a day.

And still, to this day, I see people on Facebook groups and internet forums saying 'I wouldn't have done that'. Well, the unfortunate fact for them is that unless they manage to stumble across an incredible amount of luck, they're never going to achieve wide scale commercial success with their books, because they quite simply don't have a business mindset.

Where I saw a very clear and obvious investment (and not only that, but an investment with an enormous, immediate and measurable return — something scarcer than rocking-horse poo), those authors saw a cost, or a risk. The simple truth of the matter is that there was no cost beyond bridging cashflow for a few weeks, and there was never even the smallest iota of risk.

(If you're still worrying about this concept, the truth is that you still do not have faith in data. Numbers do not lie. If you are that risk-averse that you cannot use solid data to inform your business decisions, you really should not be attempting to run a business. If this is you, at this point my advice is to put this book down and find a publisher.)

I was able to see immediately, to the minute, exactly what money my spend on ads was making me back in book sales. The second it dropped anywhere near break even, I could flick a switch, turn it all off and bank the money. It was foolproof.

(I should mention at this point that the same approach worked for me again in 2018, when I released my book *Tell Me I'm Wrong*, marketed it with

Facebook ads and made even more money, even more quickly, than I did with Her Last Tomorrow).

If you're still unsure or uneasy, let me try to break it down for you.

EXPENSES

A cost or expense is money that you spend. As simple as that. It's also called expenditure, outgoings and any number of other things. It's money that goes out from you or your business. You may well get something back in return, but there's no associated vehicle for that money to return to you with more on top.

INVESTMENTS

An investment is money that goes out with the expectation, knowledge or belief that it'll be returned with an additional profit.

In your indie author career, almost everything you spend money on will be an investment — as long as you spend it wisely.

Having a book cover professionally designed is an investment, because more people will buy a book that looks great and meets genre expectations.

Having your book professionally edited is an investment, because a better book will get better reviews and drive future sales for years to come. The feedback from your editor will also make you a better writer when you come to write future books, which will in turn make those books more successful.

Spending money on Facebook ads or other marketing is an investment, because it'll either generate direct book sales or build branding and visibility, drive mailing list signups and generally help spread the word about your books.

Going to the pub and buying a few beers is an expense. Sure, you get something from it — drunk, usually, and a divorce if things get really bad — but neither of those could be considered investments. Your cable TV subscription is also an expense. You get lots of fun from it, but you're not going to see that money again.

Spending money on advertising your books is an investment. You're doing so with the expectation, belief or even just the hope that it'll come back to you — with profit — in the form of book sales. Having a professional book cover designed is also an investment, because a great cover will increase your sales and pay for that cover designer fifty-fold in no time.

The problem many indie authors have is that even if they are able to understand the difference between an expense and an investment, they still can't bring themselves to act on that understanding. They get the logic, they know a new professionally designed cover will probably boost their book sales, but *Oh my god five hundred dollars!*

You might have noticed that this approach irks me somewhat. It's said that you have to spend money to make money. That's not strictly true. The truth is you have to invest money to make money. And the key is in looking at these supposed costs and working out which ones actually are costs and which are investments that'll benefit you in the future. After all, being an indie author is very much a long-term game.

SUMMARY POINTS

- **Have faith in data. Numbers do not lie.**
- **Expenses should not be expected to return.**
- **Investments should be expected to return.**

Yes, I know. I've spent the last few chapters talking about the importance of profit, what it is and why you shouldn't be scared of it. So why am I now throwing you this curveball?

For very good reasons.

Let me give you a scenario.

SCENARIO 1

Let's assume I'm spending $100 a day on advertising. For a while, that $100 brings me $150 in extra book sales. $50 profit every day. Fantastic, right?

Right. Absolutely. No doubt about that. But it isn't just $50 in profit, is it? It's $150 in extra book sales. If you make $2 a book, that's 75 new readers a day, 2,250 a month, 27,000 readers a year who wouldn't have bought your book otherwise. And you get $50 profit a day on top of that.

That's the ideal. But it's not the be-all-and-end-all.

Let's look at another scenario.

SCENARIO 2

Later down the line, that $100 a day on advertising is only returning $100 in sales. I'm no longer making a profit, but I'm not losing money either. Time to cut the ad? No. Why?

Because I'm still reaching 50 new readers every day. That's 1,500 new readers a month, or 18,000 new readers a year. Those people wouldn't have bought my book otherwise. But, from those 18,000 people, you can be fairly sure that a number of them will:

- Buy one of my other books (pro-tip: I wasn't lying when I told you to put this book down and write more books)
- Leave a review on the book which will help drive future sales
- Join my mailing list, giving me the opportunity to sell future books to them
- Tell their family and friends how much they loved your book, stimulating future sales

On top of that, you can be almost certain that:

- The increased sales will kickstart Amazon's algorithms, stimulating Also Boughts, driving up rank and increasing visibility (The 'Customers who bought this item also bought' section on an Amazon product page is driven by a complex algorithm based largely on sales volumes.)
- Amazon might email the reader to let them know when you've got a new book out — especially if they've chosen to 'follow' you on Amazon

So breaking even is fine. But what about if you make a loss?

SCENARIO 3

This time, I'm still spending $100 a day but only making $80 in increased sales. I'm now losing $20 a day. Not quite. At least, I wouldn't use the word 'losing'.

In this scenario, I'm reaching approximately 40 new readers every day, which is 1,200 a month or over 14,000 new readers a year.

The long-term benefits from Scenario 2 still apply. In the long-term, you'll be selling more books and extending your reach, so the long-term situation is that you're still going to be in profit. Remember the importance we put on long-term thinking versus short-term thinking earlier in the book.

Personally, I'd happily take a small short-term loss in order to lay down the foundations for my future career. Remember: this is an investment, not an expense. It's not technically a loss if it's going towards building your brand and increasing the likelihood of people buying your future books.

In this scenario, a $20 'loss' per day equates to $7,300 a year. Stick with me.

Let's say, for example, that of those 14,000 new readers the ads have brought you, only 10% like the book enough to buy one of your future books. That's 1,400 readers who'll buy your next book, meaning that title will generate an extra $2,800 a year in royalties that it wouldn't have seen otherwise.

Our 'loss' is now $4,500, effectively down from $20 a day to $12.

Let's also assume that you've got a strong page at the back of your book enticing readers to join your mailing list. Let's say a quarter of them take you up on the offer. That's 3,500 new readers on your mailing list. Even if only half of those (1,750) go on to buy your next book, that's another $3,500 the next book will earn you.

Our 'loss' is now $1,000 over the year, effectively down from $20 a day to $2.75. That's less than the cost of a cup of coffee in order to future-proof your indie author career.

Where this really starts to kick in is when you look at volume. This scenario resulting in a $1,000 loss (better than the apparent $7,300 loss a first glance would have you believe) assumes you only release one other book that year.

Those ads, although they lost money on the book you were advertising, generated $6,300 in extra sales for your second book. But what if there's a third book?

If you manage to get three books out that year, and if the same people who went on to buy book 2 also buy book 3, things look very different:

Apparent loss on book 1: -$7,300
    Extra sales on book 2: $6,300
    Effective loss across two books: -$1,000
    Extra sales on book 3: $6,300
    Effective profit across three books: $5,300

Throw a fourth book into the mix and you're over $11,000 in profit, even though your first glance at the data told you you'd suffered a loss of $7,300.

Writing and releasing four books in a year is a big ask, I know. But it's extremely achievable. And this assumes that you don't already have four books out. If you start running those ads once you've already got four books out, the hard work is done and you'll start to see that real-terms profit much more quickly

Yet again, it comes down to two things:

1. Long-term thinking is crucial
2. Write more books

And, on that note, it's time to look long-term.

SUMMARY POINTS

- **You need to think long-term.**
- **Day-to-day profit and loss does not necessarily reflect long-term benefits.**
- **Any investment in advertising and marketing is likely to yield long-term results.**
- **The more books you have out, the easier it'll be to profit in the long-term and short-term.**

PUSHING IT ON

We spoke a little earlier on about the difference between costs and investments, and why they're definitely not the same thing.

Investing isn't something that only needs to be done at the start of your career or when you've got a new book out. If you want your career to keep growing, you have to keep feeding it in the same way as you would a pet, child or plant.

Lots of authors like to reinvest a predetermined percentage of their profits or income back into their books. I know authors who look at what they've sold at the end of the month, take 50% for themselves and put 50% back into advertising and marketing, so at the end of the next month they'll have even more to divide in half.

This principle works well, but I'd suggest weighting it so that in the early stages of your career you're reinvesting everything. As things start to take off and you feel some traction, you can think about lowering those percentages. Once you're a six-figure author, you might like to reinvest 20% of your income each month, just to keep things ticking over.

Bear in mind that these numbers are more or less plucked out of the air — it's the concept and the logic behind it that I want you to focus on.

Let's assume for argument's sake that this is an easy industry (it isn't) and you can easily predict what your marketing dollars will get you (you can't).

WORKED EXAMPLE

Let's say that for every dollar you spend on marketing, you'll get $1.20 back in book sales. In your first month, you spend $100 and get $120 back. Great, huh? Let's pull that money out and do the same again!

No. Because in month two you'll have spent $100 and made another $120. At the end of month two, you've made $40 profit. Might sound great, but think what would happen if you'd put it ALL back in?

In this scenario, month two sees an investment of $120, and a return of $144. At the end of month two, you've now got $44 instead of $40 — you're 10% better off.

Let's extrapolate both scenarios across a year. In

scenario one, you invest $100 in each of the 12 months and make $120 each time.

Spend: $1,200. Revenue: $1,440. Profit: $240.

Don't forget, though, the spend is effectively only $100 of your own money, which has been reinvested each month. Similarly, the revenue is mostly that same $100 coming back to you each month.

In **scenario two**, you invest the money back in every month. In month three, your $144 makes you $172.80. Reinvesting that in month four gives you $207.36 back in book sales. By the time you get to the end of the year, the picture is quite different:

Spend: $3,958.05. Revenue: $4749.66. Profit: $791.61.

Again, you've only spent $100 of your own money, which has been reinvested each month. The only difference between the two scenarios is that you didn't take that $20 profit out each month, but reinvested it. By the end of the year you're $551.61 better off (a 229.8% increase on scenario one).

So, if you were able to hold off drawing out any money for a year and, instead, reinvested it in marketing and advertising your books, you'd be a whole lot better off. Now imagine how different that picture would look if we were talking thousands instead of hundreds of dollars.

Of course, you'll need to draw money out at some point. But this illustrates the point I made earlier — that reinvesting everything in the early days will leave you in a much better position further down the line.

To compare, the position you'd be in at the end of the year in scenario two would take you three years and four months to better using scenario one. You'd be three years and four months further behind in your career, all for twenty bucks a month.

As a point of note, after three years and four months the author following scenario two would have earned almost $16,500 in royalties in that month alone.

I know the science isn't exact and that no-one can guarantee making back exactly $1.20 for every $1 spent, but that extremely modest profit margin does a good job of illustrating the principle behind what I'm saying, and perfectly displays the power of reinvesting and building on your foundations.

SUMMARY POINTS

- Re-investing what you earn can reap huge rewards in the long run.
- In the early stages of your career, reinvest everything.
- As you start to see real positive traction, take out some money but don't reduce your investment if things are going well.

We touched earlier on the power of residuals, and how you need to think long-term about your indie author career.

In the same way as it'd be wrong to think of a book as needing to make you instant income, it would also be wrong to think of a book as a single product.

It's widely believed that once a book is written, all an indie author needs to do is put it live on Amazon, maybe get a print-on-demand paperback sorted, then move on to the next book. If that's your attitude, you're leaving money on the table.

The simple fact is that your one book can actually form multiple non-competing products which will bring you extra income. If you write fiction, we're generally talking:

EBOOKS

Distributed either through Amazon Kindle, or Kindle plus Kobo, iBooks, NOOK, Google Play et al.

PAPERBACKS

These should not be ignored. A huge number of readers still consume paperbacks, and it's effectively free to publish your paperback using KDP Print or CreateSpace, although you will have to pay a small fee to your cover designer to adapt your ebook cover for print. I also recommend using Ingram Spark to give your books a chance of being ordered in by high-street stores and libraries.

HARDBACKS AND LARGE PRINT

Using Ingram Spark also opens up new avenues of possibility, such as offering hardback copies of your books and large-print paperbacks. Large-print books are increasing in popularity, particularly as many voracious readers are older people.

One of the most popular reasons people buy e-readers is that they can increase the font size to something they feel is comfortable. Libraries are choosing to order large-print books because library customers tend to be on the older end of the age spectrum and *anyone* can read a large-print book, whereas books printed with a smaller font size can only be read by a certain number of people.

That's another example of thinking smart and ensuring your books can be read by as many people as possible.

AUDIOBOOKS

Audiobooks are a popular and growing market, albeit nowhere near as large as many sections of the industry media have been claiming (I've seen 'Next year is the year of the audiobook!' headlines every December since 2008).

Generally speaking, having an audiobook produced via ACX (Audiobook Creation Exchange — an Amazon company) is your best option.

As well as the standard pay-upfront model of production, they also offer a royalty-share arrangement (with no up-front production fees), but this will tie you into a seven-year exclusivity contract. And trust me, I know from experience they're extremely expensive to get out of.

If you're going down the audio route, I'd recommend paying upfront for your production. The industry is currently in a state of flux, with Kobo and other companies introducing audiobook platforms which could make ACX exclusivity a bad place to be.

At the moment, I'm not producing new audiobooks for my fiction works. At the time of writing

I've spent tens of thousands on audiobook production and they still haven't turned a profit. However, many people make good money from them so it's a decision you'll have to weigh up for yourself.

I do, however, intend to have this book produced in audio, purely because I'm reliably informed that non-fiction audio sells better than fiction audio.

BOX SETS

When I write and release book 4 in a series, I immediately package up the first three books, add some bonus material such as a couple of short stories and release the package as a new product, priced around 40% lower than all three books would cost separately.

This has been common practice in the industry for a long time now, and readers love it. It allows them to get hold of more books at a lower price, and it's good news for authors too.

The logic is perverse. Surely, if the reader wanted the books that badly they'd buy them all separately anyway and you'd make more money, right?

Wrong.

My own experiments and those of almost every other prominent indie author have yielded the same results. My Knight & Culverhouse box set of books 1 to 3 has become my third biggest-selling title of all time (after only *Her Last Tomorrow* and *Tell Me I'm*

Wrong). Despite that, sales of the individual books have not dropped. In fact, they've risen.

Box sets are a fantastic way to add a new product to your catalogue and make a lot of extra money with minimal effort.

Once you've created your box set, don't forget to create a paperback version (usually one large paperback with all of the books contained within the one cover) and an audiobook version. Audiobook boxsets are particularly popular, as audio customers often get one free book a month. Choosing a box set is far better value for them, and the author makes far more money as audio royalties are determined by book length.

TRANSLATIONS AND FOREIGN RIGHTS

Don't forget that English isn't the only language that books are published in. Translations and foreign rights are big business, but it's not something you'll want to try to tackle on your own.

You'll need an agency to actively work on selling these rights for you. Yes, they'll take a small cut, but would you know how to negotiate a beneficial publishing contract with an Estonian publisher? Authors shouldn't even consider negotiating a contract with an English publisher on their own.

My books have been translated into numerous languages. It took me absolutely no time or effort whatsoever and brings me free money each month. What's not to love?

As mentioned earlier in the book, finding a specialist agent (see the Writers and Artists' Yearbook for recommended agents) is the recommended way to go. If you have foreign publishers or film and TV producers knocking at your door already, the Society of Authors and Alliance of Independent Authors can both provide contractual advice.

FILM AND TV RIGHTS

This might seem like a long way off, but you'd be surprised how many books are optioned for film and TV every year. Mostly people think it's unrealistic for them because they've not tried.

Again, you'll need an agency to try to sell the rights for you, but it's well worth the time and effort.

If you're fortunate enough that a production company does buy the rights or option on your books, congratulations, but please don't celebrate too hard. Your chances of the film or TV series actually being made are still in the region of 1%, but you're a lot closer than you were before and you'll likely receive a relatively small but not insubstantial annual retainer for the company keeping first refusal on the rights.

If you're not writing in the realms of fiction but instead write non-fiction, your income streams can be extended further:

WORKBOOKS

These, I'm reliably informed by people who know a lot more about this sort of thing than me, are essentially repackaged versions of non-fiction books with additional questions and exercises, including additional space for the reader to fill in their own notes.

These are a great idea for non-fiction writers and readers alike, as they're an extra product for the writer to sell and a fantastic way of the reader improving their learning. That's why people take notes in lectures — because the act of writing down the information doubles up that storage power in your memory.

When Sacha Black wrote her non-fiction book *13 Steps To Evil: How to Craft Superbad Villains*, she released a workbook alongside it in which she took a summary of each chapter, then added a list of questions which would help the reader practice and develop that facet of their fictional villain. The workbook was formatted with blank spaces for the reader to write in the answers. Furthermore, it gives her an additional stream of income without having to carry out lots of extra work.

Sacha then created a series page for her non-fiction titles at Amazon. After claiming the series page through Author Central, she saw a huge spike in her workbook sales due to its new increased visibility.

This is something other prominent non-fiction writers, such as Joanna Penn, do to great effect. Indeed, Joanna Penn is the go-to person when it comes to using your books to open up multiple income streams.

COURSES

These are becoming more and more popular for non-fiction writers. Platforms such as Teachable allow experts to create an online course, which potential students can pay to access.

Courses are usually pre-prepared using video modules as well as PDF worksheets and other materials that might be useful to learning.

As someone who's been involved in the production of one of these courses (I produced and presented the *BookBub Ads for Authors* module in Mark Dawson's famous *Ads For Authors* course), I can attest to the fact that it's a *lot* of hard work. It's not just the production — it's the marketing and administration that goes with running a course. However, if you don't mind the extra legwork, these can be pretty lucrative.

SPEAKING

Once your name starts to get out there, you'll likely be invited to speak at literary festivals and events. These are lots of fun, but don't have that many tangible advantages.

Many festivals will ask you to speak for free, citing increased book sales and exposure as potential benefits. Speaking with a decade of experience, I can tell you this is largely rubbish. Even if you do rock up with a car full of books (and I generally don't, because…) you'll probably only sell a small handful at best, and the money you make will not even cover your time.

The Society of Authors has a set of guidelines for festival and speaking fees, which I strongly feel all festivals and events should adhere to. I have friends who run literary festivals and, of course, I understand that it's very difficult for festivals and events to make money and that budgets are tight, but something rather sticks in the throat when it comes to organised events which claim to exist to support and promote authors, but which conversely expects them to work for free.

I've spoken at some huge literary festivals, including to an absolutely packed-out audience at the world-famous London Book Fair, and I've seen no increase in book sales from any of them. They're great fun, but they're only going to be worthwhile if you're being paid for your time.

If you're a non-fiction writer, you could make money speaking to businesses or groups of people who might be receptive to your content. For example, if your book is about being a motivational manager, you could arrange to visit companies and deliver a talk to their management, perhaps throwing in a few free copies of your book too.

Shelley Wilson is a non-fiction author who does this to great effect. She told me:

> As an indie author, it's imperative that you network within your chosen industry/genre. I write non-fiction personal development books where my ideal readers are mid-life women. I found that joining women's only business networking groups gets me in front of my target audience.
>
> From this face-to-face interaction, I've been able to build a series of workshops, eCourses, and talks around the theme of my books and my writing career and secure regular paid work as a consultant for those business owners. By having the opportunity to meet and engage with my audience in person I remain at the forefront of their mind and receive many recommendations.

SUMMARY POINTS

- A book is not a single product.
- One book can become multiple products.
- Diversifying your income streams is crucial to long-term success.
- Launching complementary formats and products is essentially free money.
- Non-fiction authors have even more potential income streams open to them.

ADVERTISING AND MARKETING

WHY MARKETING AND ADVERTISING DON'T TURN A PROFIT

Lots of books go into detail about the difference between marketing and advertising. The more the subject gets discussed, the more the lines get blurred and they essentially become the same thing.

If you want to have *some* distinction, advertising is technically part of the larger marketing pie, but it really makes absolutely no difference whatsoever. Call a horse a sheep and it'll still neigh and have a bloody good go at winning the Grand National.

For our purposes, it's all about building awareness of our brand and books, finding new readers and making it more likely that potential readers will buy our books. You can call it whatever you like, but that's the aim of the game. A builder who's never been told his hammer is called a hammer still knows it's used for whacking nails into stuff.

The marketing umbrella for authors includes many different activities, including, but certainly not limited to:

- Email marketing
- Social media
- Back-of-book content
- Street teams and social influencers
- Facebook, BookBub or AMS advertising
- Festivals and speaking events
- Traditional PR (TV, radio, newspapers, magazines)
- Offline advertising

Of course, the list could go on. Telling family and friends about your books could count as marketing. Anything that is intended or likely to increase awareness of your books and ideally convert people into readers counts as a marketing activity. Advertising is just one of these factors.

If you've delved into the depths of any of the many indie author groups on Facebook, or even some of the more popular web forums, you'll probably be aware that authors tend to obsess over whether their advertising is turning a profit. You'll hear ROI and profit being thrown about as the only things that matter. And they are. Up to a point.

Traditionally, advertising and marketing never

turn a profit. That's not the objective of the exercise. Do you think McDonald's put an advert on TV then try to calculate exactly how many McFlurrys they sold as a direct consequence of that ad? No, of course they don't. They're building and reinforcing a brand, making you more likely to head into their premises when you're faced with the option of McDonald's and a burger joint you've never heard of.

This is the beauty of advertising and marketing as a *branding* exercise. But more on that later.

As indie authors, we are very fortunate to be able to track the success of our ads. We can see — more or less on the same day — whether our ads are working and selling more books for us. Even major traditional publishers don't have the same power, as their reporting tends to be done in quarters and they have to account for returns, spoilage and various other factors which don't affect indies.

In the next chapter, we'll look at this in some more detail.

SUMMARY POINTS

- **Marketing is about building awareness of your brand.**
- **Everything except writing is marketing.**
- **Marketing and advertising aren't**

traditionally designed to turn a direct profit.
- Indie authors are able to track direct profit — something even traditional publishers can't do as effectively.

The question you might be asking yourself now, as you think about using your new business mindset to form a marketing plan, is does it matter that your marketing doesn't need to turn a direct profit?

The answer is both yes and no. There are many reasons why and situations in which your marketing and advertising *do* need to turn a direct profit:

WE AREN'T MADE OF MONEY

I used the example of McDonald's a little earlier, but it would be fair to say that indie authors can't be compared to McDonald's when it comes to either income or advertising budgets. We can't afford to spend lots of money on branding and keeping our names in people's minds on the off-chance that they *might* buy one of our books at some indeterminate point in the future.

IT'S A CRAPSHOOT

If you can't measure success, how do you know whether or not your marketing is working? The only measure you'll have is whether or not you're selling more books on average this time next year than you are right now, and by then you'll be down a whole year's marketing budget. That's far too speculative for even the most ambitious author.

BOOKS ARE IMPULSE PURCHASES

By rights, it's a whole lot easier to sell a book to someone who's never heard of you than it is to sell them a car or a fridge-freezer. Books are impulse purchases. If someone sees a book they like the look of, they're far more likely to take a chance on it than they are on most other products. After all, what's a few dollars for a week's entertainment and a potentially life-changing experience?

Having said that, there are also a number of arguments in favour of *not* obsessing over direct profit:

ONLY ADVERTISING FOR PROFIT MAKES ALL ADVERTISING HARDER

When you market and advertise for branding and awareness, you're laying down the foundations for future books and products and will make life easier for yourself in the long run.

If you release a book six months down the line and your potential readers have heard your name dozens of times, they're far more likely to buy your book when it's out. Going straight to direct sales ads means you've got a lot more work to do to convince them to buy your book, because they've never heard of you.

Remember the seven touches principle of marketing. Potential customers need to see or hear about your product up to seven times before considering buying it.

IT'S NOT ALL ABOUT PROFIT!

I'm saying this again here, because it's super relevant.

Long-term thinking is crucial. It's not all about turning an immediate day-to-day profit, although that is, of course, a huge bonus if you can make it happen.

Your advertising and marketing will be increasing visibility and making people aware of your books, making them more likely to buy in the future. And those who *do* buy will likely:

- Buy one of your other books
- Leave a review on the book which will help drive future sales
- Join your mailing list, giving you the opportunity to sell future books to them
- Tell their family and friends how much they loved your book, stimulating future sales

You'll also stimulate Amazon's algorithms as your books get more eyes on them, showing Amazon that your books are becoming more and more popular.

This is what's known as the **halo effect** — those ancillary, tertiary things which help to drive and build your author career off the back of your marketing and advertising. Many of them are things which can't be measured, but which are undeniably there and which will be a huge boost to you in the long-term.

SUMMARY POINTS

- Direct, short-term profit is important but not crucial.
- Think long-term.
- There are many other benefits to advertising and marketing other than direct profit — this is known as the halo effect.

DATA

THE IMPORTANCE OF DATA

I really cannot overstate the importance of data. Facts and statistics are the only things you can use to measure your success and whether your efforts are working.

After all, how would you possibly know if your marketing and advertising were successful if you weren't able to see how many books you were selling? That number of books sold is data, albeit very simple and basic data.

In writing this section of the book, I spoke to Brian Meeks, a fellow author who is obsessed with data. To him, data is everything. It informs every decision he makes. He told me:

A woman reached out to me. She was frustrated because the changes we had made to her description didn't work. She had fewer sales after than before.

Her old description was horrible.

I didn't believe her.

I did believe that she had simply compared the before sales to the after sales. And I knew immediately what the problem was, but I wanted her to see where she had gone wrong. This type of poor analysis causes authors everywhere to make devastatingly bad decisions that crush their bottom line.

I asked her, "Did you compare your number of ad clicks before and after?"

"No."

"Do you understand why you need to do that?"

"Not really."

"If you had a lot more clicks before and your ads have died, then what would happen to your sales regardless of the description change?"

"Oh, I see what you mean."

We did the math and her description conversion was much better with the new description than the old one.

If she had not reached out to me, she would have probably lived with her horrible description for months or years to come. When her clicks grew again, her conversion would still be around 1:30. The new one was closer to 1:14. (Note: a great description will convert at 1:8 to 1:10, so we still had some testing to do to get it perfect, but it was much better than the old one.)

She would have gotten half the conversions.

That equals a lot of money.

What's your point, Brian?

You need to keep your data.

But data is like math. And math makes me weep. Can't I just…

No, you can't just anything…you must keep track of your sales, impressions, clicks, downloads (from free promotions), dates you ran newsletter swaps, dates you made changes to your covers or descriptions, or anything else that may be needed to analyze your book.

I know that's a long list.

I know you don't believe me.

But you are running a business. It's important. And the analysis, even if you are a math phobe, isn't as tough as you might think. It can be learned.

It will be the secret sauce that takes you to the next level.

Please track your data.

It's worth it.

BRIAN MEEKS

Now, I'm not saying that to be a successful indie

author you're going to have to be a data nerd, but to be a successful indie author you're going to have to be a data nerd.

I know. I know. I never used to be one either. But once I discovered that spending an hour or two setting up some spreadsheets could multiply my monthly income over the course of the year, I became something of a convert.

I have spreadsheets that track everything. Literally everything. Each month, as a matter of course, I log the number of reviews and average star rating for each book. I log the number of copies sold on each platform and the income generated from them. I log my number of mailing list subscribers, Twitter followers and Facebook followers. This allows me to make sure everything's heading in the right direction and identify areas in which I'm falling behind.

On a more granular level, when I'm running Facebook ads I log information daily. Each morning after 8am UK time I open my spreadsheet, then log into Facebook Ads Manager, and each of the vendors I distribute through. (8am UK time is midnight on the west coast of the United States, and generally means that — in terms of 99% of sales — the previous day is officially over.)

I log:

- how much was spent on advertising the previous day,

- how many clicks that got me, and
- what money was earned from each vendor.

The formulae I've set up in my spreadsheet then tell me my average cost-per-click, profit, ROI, buy rate, average cost per sale and what my effective maximum cost-per-click is. Each of these formulae is just a bit of basic mathematics calculated using the data Facebook and the vendors provide me.

Now, please don't obsess over these terms or panic if you don't know what they mean. That'll all be covered in another, more marketing-specific book. For now, I'm just giving you a brief overview of what I do so you can see how valuable it is and how this approach and mindset could transform your career, too.

Here are some simple formulae you can use to calculate data and turn it into information:

Cost per click = Money spent / clicks achieved
Buy rate (BTR) = Sales achieved / clicks achieved (expressed as a percentage)
Cost per sale = Money spent / sales achieved
Effective max CPC = Royalty per sale x BTR

That data then feeds into another spreadsheet which tells me how much money I've made on each platform through advertising in previous months, and also projects across the current month so I can see what I'm likely to make this month. This allows me to plan ahead.

Let's have a look at a worked example so you can see what data Facebook and Amazon provide to us, and what information we can glean from that.

WORKED EXAMPLE

Let's assume that one day I spend £71.76 on Facebook advertising (data provided by Facebook). That money gets me 887 clicks (data provided by Facebook) and makes me £322.93 in 188 sales (data provided by Amazon).

That's about the extent of the useful data either Facebook or Amazon provide, but there's a LOT we can do with that.

For example:

- I can minus £71.76 spend from £322.93 revenue and discover I made £251.17 in **profit**.
- I can divide this profit by the spend and discover I made 350% **ROI**.
- I can divide £71.76 spend by 887 clicks and discover each click cost me 8p (**CPC**).
- I can divide my 188 sales by my 887 clicks and discover that 21.2% of people clicking the ad bought the book (**BTR**).

- I can divide my £71.76 spend by my 188 sales and discover that each sale cost me 38p (**CPS**).
- I can multiply my royalty rate by my 21.2% BTR to find out that anything under 37p CPC should yield a profit (my **effective max CPC**).

This is all extremely simple arithmetic. All of that information comes from four simple numbers provided by Facebook and Amazon (spend, clicks, revenue, sales) and the minus, divide and multiply functions. Nothing heavy, even for a mathsphobe like me.

You can now use your effective max CPC to see easily whether your ads are likely to be profiting or not, see how much a sale costs you to achieve in terms of advertising spend and know what percentage of ad clickers actually go on to buy your book. This information is crucial to informing your future business and marketing decisions.

As you can see, the power of data is extraordinary. Please, please don't underestimate data. It's free, it's simple and it could revolutionise the way you make decisions.

SUMMARY POINTS

- Data is important.
- Data is very important.
- Brian Meeks knows what he's talking about.

CONCLUSION

WHERE NOW?

In a way, I'm kind of hoping you didn't get to this chapter.

There are a handful of books which completely changed my mindset or gave me epiphanies, and every single time I've thrown the book down immediately and rushed to my laptop to run some ads, work on my marketing or write a few more chapters of my own books.

I've included a list of those books in the Recommended Reading chapter, at the end of this book.

I hope this book can have a similar impact on you. Either way, thank you for sticking with it.

There is so much I wanted to say, but had to rein in for the sake of brevity. I didn't want this book to be a weighty, daunting tome which new authors would be afraid to tackle. I wanted it to be a tight, concise kick up the backside for authors at all stages of their careers. I hope I've achieved that.

Some sections had to be tackled carefully. Any mentions of marketing, advertising and data needed to be carefully managed. I'm well aware of my reputation for being good at advertising and marketing, and I know many people will have wanted more 'juice' on those topics, but this book is about one thing and one thing only: **mindset**.

Where possible, I've tried to allude to concepts such as marketing, advertising and data within the scope of how mindset affects them. Advertising and marketing tactics are a whole different ball game, and a subject for another time. Mindset is the basis of everything, and therefore must come first.

Mindset is a difficult thing to get across. It's rather like trying to teach someone how to ride a bike through the medium of a non-fiction book.

I've gradually come to realise that everything I do in the non-fiction sphere — be it books, courses, podcasts, webinars or talks — has mindset at its core. Even if I'm teaching practical tips about marketing or advertising, I find myself backing up my tips with a basis in mindset.

It's at the centre of everything I do. The principles of *The Indie Author Mindset* inform every decision I make, and provide a fundamental, clear direction for my career. Once the mindset is achieved and understood, everything else falls into place.

I sincerely hope that you've felt a 'click' whilst reading this book. If you haven't, please take a few days, perhaps weeks, then read it again. Once you feel that cog dropping into place, you're there. And everything you do from here on in will seem natural and comfortable.

I sincerely wish you all the best, wherever you are on your self-publishing journey.

If you're an established author, you'll know it is fun, rewarding and humbling. At times it's also difficult, painful and crushing.

If you're a new author, you'll likely feel daunted, inspired, nervous and excited all at the same time. That doesn't change. Those feelings are what I feel every single day. Take heart in the knowledge that you're already there. Your mind is now in the right place.

For those of you who want to continue your journey, you can join me and other likeminded authors in the official Indie Author Mindset Facebook Group, at https://www.facebook.com/groups/IndieAuthorMindset/.

I welcome feedback, suggestions and questions. Please email me at mindset@adamcroft.net if you're left with any questions or if you want any help with anything. I'll always do all I can to help, although it may take me a few days to reply at busy times.

But, above all, have fun. This is a fantastically rewarding industry for those who approach it in the right way. If you apply the principles outlined in this book, you'll have a fantastic foundation for your career.

I wish you all the very best with it.

In writing this book, it became abundantly clear to me that there is much, much more I can say and do to help authors at all stages of their careers.

A lot of it just doesn't belong in this book. I've tried to keep this book as tight as possible and to only focus on the psychological and mindset aspects, which will form the bedrock for everything you do from now on.

Since I started writing this book I've built up a list of nine more non-fiction books which will help indie authors to kick their careers on to the next level. However, I'm adamant that the content of this book had to remain undiluted.

If you're interested in any future books I write for authors, please click here to join my mailing list: http://adamcroft.net/nonfiction.

I'll email you when I have new books available

and, as a thank-you for joining, you'll get an exclusive discount off the launch price of each book.

And please check out the official Facebook group at https://www.facebook.com/groups/IndieAuthorMindset/.

Thank you once again for reading *The Indie Author Mindset*.

Adam Croft
July 2018

RESOURCES

This is a non-exhaustive list of books which have either been referenced in *The Indie Author Mindset*, or which I highly recommend as further reading.

Write. Publish. Repeat.
Johnny B. Truant, Sean Platt, David Wright
A no-holds-barred kick-up-the-arse guide to productive writing and publishing.

The War of Art
Steven Pressfield
Motivational lessons for writers at the beginning of their careers, or those who've found themselves in a slump.

How to Write a Sizzling Synopsis
Bryan Cohen

One of the easiest ways to boost your book sales is to optimise your blurb or product description. Bryan shows you how.

Strangers to Superfans
David Gaughran
A comprehensive guide to turning a potential reader into a die-hard fan, enabling you to take advantage of vital word-of-mouth marketing.

Mastering Amazon Ads
Brian Meeks
This book is aimed more towards advertising, but from a totally data-driven perspective. It's a great guide to the principles of working with and trusting data.

Printed in Great Britain
by Amazon

37420246R00139